Ro
The
bec

compare to the joy thats coming -

He's working while you are waiting + worrying!

How to Study the Bible

By Dr. Chuck Missler

How to Study the Bible

Published by Koinonia House
P.O. Box D
Coeur d'Alene, ID 83816-0347
www.khouse.org

Author: Dr. Chuck Missler
Editor: Amy Joy

ISBN: 978-1-57821-724-3

All Scripture quotations are from the King James Version of the Holy Bible.

PRINTED IN THE UNITED STATES OF AMERICA

Table of Contents

Chapter 1
The Word of God

And that from a child thou hast known the holy scriptures, which are able to make thee wise unto salvation through faith which is in Christ Jesus.

2 Timothy 3:15

The Bible is the Word of God.

That's quite a statement. If we really believe that, it should change everything. We realize that the Bible is not the random jottings of ancient Hebrew sages, but a portal - a portal into the heart of our Creator. The Word of God is given to instruct and correct and guide us[1], but it is also a weapon to protect us from the enemy of our souls.[2]

For the word of God is quick, and powerful, and sharper than any two-edged sword, piercing even to the dividing asunder of soul and spirit, and of the joints and marrow, and is a discerner of the thoughts and intents of the heart.

Hebrews 4:12

The Bible is by far the best-selling book of all time, yet thousands of Bibles sit on shelves year after year gathering dust. When we come to realize the true nature of the Bible, we understand what a terrible waste that is. We live in a world filled with deception, and the best way to recognize a lie is to already know the truth. We need to *know* this book that God breathed through His prophets and disciples. We need to know what it says and how to wield it in our own lives. I often say that the Bible is a message by one Author from outside our time domain, but it's vital to know why I say that and how it's true.

How should we study the Bible? I'm going to make some personal remarks in this book. I've been studying the Bible for more than sixty years, so I've developed my own viewpoints on matters. However, nobody should accept anything just because I've said it or because some other Bible teacher has said it. You have a much better tutor than me readily available to you through the person of the Holy Spirit. Research and study the Bible for yourself to determine what it says - from front to back. My foundational verse on Bible study is Acts 17:11, which tells us about the people of Berea, who:

> *...were more noble than those in Thessalonica, in that they received the word with all readiness of mind, and searched the scriptures daily, whether those things were so."*
>
> Acts 17:11

We are in a predicament as human beings. We are plagued by a general spiritual blindness. Most of us cannot see past the atoms of this world into the dimensions beyond us, the dimensions of angels and demons, or of the spiritual warfare that takes place on our behalf. We get a peek in 2 Kings 6 and Daniel 10, but we cannot see the full reality ourselves.

Too many of us think of Jesus Christ as that broken carpenter hanging on a cross. We do not fully appreciate that the man who rose again on Resurrection Sunday is the King of the universe, through whom all things were made. (John 1:3) As we study the Bible, our greatest discovery will be a growing appreciation for the person and identity of Jesus, the Messiah of Israel and Creator and Lord of all things.

The Age of Deceit

It has become increasingly politically incorrect to be a Bible believer. It's strange to realize that many church congregations are embarrassed by people who take the Bible seriously. Our culture is apathetic to the very idea of truth. It used to be the dream of American mothers and fathers for their children to go off to college and learn, to become good thinkers and moral people able to distinguish right from wrong. Today, students go to college to be told there is no right and wrong. They are told, "You have your truth and I have mine." The value of relativism has had tragic consequences.

Satan was a liar and a murderer from the beginning (John 8:44), and his goal is to deceive us. The only remedy, the only inoculation we can get to protect us from deceit is for us to do our homework. Benjamin Franklin is often misquoted as saying, "a jack of all trades and a master of none." It's actually, "a jack of all trades and a master of one." In other words, an educated person should know a little about everything, but know everything about one thing. If we are Christians, we should be a master of the Bible. We should know it inside and out. As Christians, we don't just represent ourselves. We are ambassadors for Jesus Christ, and it's vital that we represent Him faithfully. We cannot do that well if we do not know the Bible - and not just parts of the Bible taken out of context, but the Bible as a whole.

It's my premise that we cannot understand God's Word by spending 45 minutes at it once a week listening to a sermon (which may or may not dig into the Bible at all).We need to be involved in dedicated personal study.

Prerequisites to Study:

I'm going to suggest there are a couple of preconditions you should have in place before you start your study of God's Word. These are important. We want to get all we can out of our Bible study. We don't want it to be a dry lump of wordy onion-skin papers that hit us in the face but don't dig deep into our hearts and souls.

First, ask Jesus Christ to be Lord of your life. This is vital, because when the Holy Spirit comes and dwells in us, He is the one who leads us into all truth. In John 3, Jesus told Nicodemus that he had to be born again, and that applies to all of us. People who aren't saved can read the Bible and learn from it, but it's the Holy Spirit who brings the Bible to life in our minds and hearts:

> *Even the Spirit of truth; whom the world cannot receive, because it seeth him not, neither knoweth him: but ye know him; for he dwelleth with you, and shall be in you.*
>
> John 14:17

> *But when the Comforter is come, whom I will send unto you from the Father, even the Spirit of truth, which proceedeth from the Father, he shall testify of me:*
>
> John 15:26

> *Howbeit when he, the Spirit of truth, is come, he will guide you into all truth: for he shall not speak of himself; but whatsoever he shall hear, that shall he speak: and he will shew you things to come.*
>
> John 16:13

Many people don't realize that God *wants* to give us the Holy Spirit, just as a father wants to give his children good things. We need His Spirit, and He is more than willing to fill us. We just have to ask.

> *For every one that asketh receiveth; and he that seeketh findeth; and to him that knocketh it shall be opened. If a son shall ask bread of any of you that is a father, will he give him a stone? or if he ask a fish, will he for a fish give him a serpent? Or if he shall ask an egg, will he offer him a scorpion? If ye then, being evil, know how to give good gifts unto your children: how much more shall your heavenly Father give the Holy Spirit to them that ask him?*
>
> Luke 11:10-13

We might have a big experience when the Holy Spirit comes to dwell in us - we might feel His love and power fill us. Or, we might not feel anything at all - yet the Holy Spirit is there, ready to do His work in us. Either way, we know that His presence is one request God will absolutely honor when we ask, because it is always good.

A second precondition is that we should always open our Bible study with prayer. It's important to remember that Bible study is a spiritual issue as well as an intellectual one. God gave us brains, and He wants us to use the minds He gave us, but we are also on a spiritual battlefield. We should always open with prayer.

A third part of preparation is obedience. We want to be under the tutorship of the Author of the Bible. God will reward our obedience with further insights. Obedience is a prerequisite, and we want to be pre-committed and surrendered to Jesus Christ as we embark on this study.

As we begin this study, let's take these things to heart. Let's bow our hearts as we begin on this little adventure.

> *Father, we pray for this moment in time. We know that there's no accidents in Your kingdom, and we simply pray that Your purpose would be accomplished in these chapters. Please open our understanding to Your Word, that this time might yield the fruit that You would intend. Please open our eyes to see the things You have for us, and give us discernment. We commit our studies and all of ourselves into Your hands, in Jesus Christ, amen.*

Chapter 2
No Shadow of Turning

Scientific explanations are always changing. That's the reality of science. As more information comes in, the stories change. Nothing is ever 100% proven in science, and all scientists know this. It was once thought that the speed of light was infinite, until the 17th century Danish astronomer Ole Rømer discovered from his observations of Jupiter's moon Io that light had a finite speed. If we compare a physics course using 1950s textbooks to a physics course today, the differences would surprise us. Neanderthals have long been regarded as hulking, stupid cave dwellers, but archeological finds have demonstrated that Neanderthals were as intelligent as modern humans (if not more so).[3]

Unlike scientific "facts," the truth never changes. That might seem an odd thing to say, but scientific facts are based on our limited observations and knowledge about the world, and truth is based on reality itself. Our understanding might change, but the truth never does. What's more important, God never changes. There is no variableness in Him - no "shadow of turning."[4] Jesus Christ is the same yesterday, today, and forever.[5]

What does that mean for us? It means that God is dependable. It means He doesn't stop being who He is. His love is everlasting, and so is His Word. His promises three thousand years ago still stand today. Our circumstances change. Our culture changes. The world changes, but God doesn't. In the 8th century B.C., Isaiah declared that God's Word lasts forever, and nearly 900 years later, the apostle Peter affirmed that truth:

> *The grass withereth, the flower fadeth: but the word of our God shall stand for ever.*
>
> Isaiah 40:8

> *For all flesh is as grass, and all the glory of man as the flower of grass. The grass withereth, and the flower thereof falleth away: But the word of the Lord endureth for ever. And this is the word which by the gospel is preached unto you.*
>
> 1 Peter 1:24-25

God accomplishes His purposes in His time - in "the fullness of time" - but He accomplishes them. When Jesus fulfilled a multitude of Old Testament prophecies, He was fulfilling promises that God had given 400-4000 years earlier. When we consider that 2000 years have passed since Christ's birth, remember that God gave a ram in Isaac's place on Mt. Moriah as a type of Christ nearly 2100 years before Jesus was born.[6] God exists outside of time. A thousand years are as a day in the eyes of God.[7]

The Bible is filled with end-times prophecies about Israel, yet 200 years ago there was no nation of Israel. Scholars habitually allegorized those prophecies, because Israel hadn't existed as a nation since the early years of the Roman Empire. Then in 1948, Israel declared its independence. Within a century, Jerusalem went from being a dingy backwash part of the Ottoman Empire to a cup of trembling for all the nations of the world. Suddenly, the ancient prophecies about end-times Israel came to life again.

Yet, the purposes in God's heart never changed. He never changed. Our limited perspectives got a step up in 1948, but the God of the universe, the King of eternity knew during all those intervening centuries exactly what He had in store for Israel and for the salvation of the whole world.

As we read the Bible, we need to remember that God doesn't change. His power, His love, His goodness and truth have everything to do with His unchanging character and very little to do with physical appearances. We live in a broken world doomed for ultimate destruction. We are faced daily with spiritual warfare that can hide its face behind the physical bodies that cry out in front of us. Yet, the Bible blazes the constant light of salvation to our dying world. We need to know it. We need to study it and understand it as our source of spiritual food.

During the middle of World War II, two Dutch sisters managed to smuggle a Bible into the Nazi's Ravensbruck concentration camp. Corrie ten Boom relates that time in her 1971 book *The Hiding Place*, saying:

> *From morning until lights-out, whenever we were not in ranks for roll call, our Bible was the center of an ever-widening circle of help and hope. Like waifs clustered around a blazing fire, we gathered about it, holding out our hearts to its warmth and light. The blacker the night around us grew, the brighter and truer and more beautiful burned the word of God.*

When we grasp the truth of the Bible and then obey it, it always leads to more truth. Most people are spiritually starved, and they don't even know what the Bible says. They believe the propaganda campaign against it. They believe the lie that God is a violent, cruel, capricious being - or they believe the lie that He is a big soft, Santa Claus character in the clouds. A love for the Bible requires knowing the Bible - and knowing the Bible leads us to a fuller, truer and greater knowledge of God. Ultimately, knowing God leads to loving and adoring Him. When we discover how truly good and wise God is - when we discover His incredible strength and love - we can hardly help but grab hold of Him with all our hearts.

The Holographic Bible

One interesting characteristic of the Bible is its holographic nature. Holograms are two or three-dimensional projections, and they're neat because you can walk around a hologram and look on top of it and under it and see all the detail.

Holography is very interesting. It's a way of capturing an image without lenses. To create a 3D hologram, we place a photographic film in front of a three-dimensional object. Then we illuminate the film with a laser and we also reflect the laser so that it also illuminates the object. What is then recorded on the film is the interference pattern caused by the object. After the film is processed in a dark room, we can hold it up to the natural light, and it looks like a dark room mistake. It's a cloudy piece of film. It appears that something went wrong - until we illuminate the film with the laser that created it in the first place. It's then that we discover the cloudy piece of film is a window into a three-dimensional space.

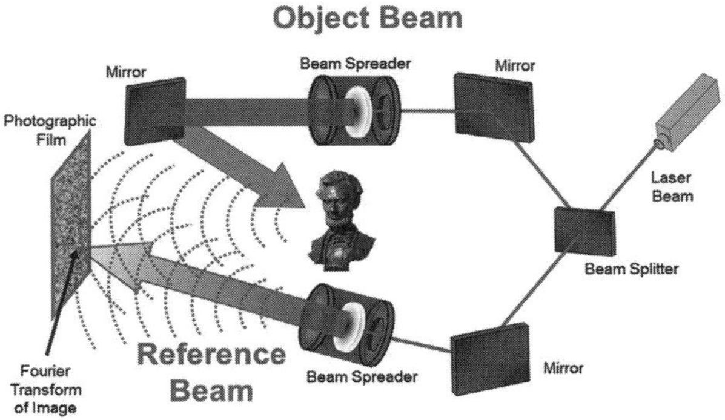

Object Beam
Mirror
Beam Spreader
Mirror
Photographic Film
Laser Beam
Beam Splitter
Reference Beam
Beam Spreader
Mirror
Fourier Transform of Image

Holograms have some very peculiar qualities. The information for that three-dimensional image is spread out over the entire film. This means that if we chop out of a piece of the holographic film, we don't lose the whole picture. The picture gets less sharp and clear, but the 3D image remains.

The same is true of the Bible. There's no single part of the Bible that talks about salvation, or obedience, or baptism, or praise. God cleverly spread all the most important topics over a wide range of books and passages. Holography is a form of recording that also anticipates hostile jamming. The major doctrines of the Bible are spread out across the entire book, and this design anticipates attacks. If we lose a chapter or a book, the picture isn't as crisp and clear, but the entire message remains.

What's more, we can only really *see* the picture when it's illuminated by the Light that created it in the first place. If we read the Bible in natural light, it sounds like a bunch of quaint tribal legends and traditions. When God Himself illuminates it for us, though, we can see His heart and His eternal plan.

A Supernatural Origin

The Bible was not written to please methodical scientists, yet it clearly anticipates technologies that we are finally seeing today. Matthew 24:22 speaks of a time of tribulation on the earth so severe that no flesh would survive if God didn't shorten those days. That statement was unfathomable in the 1900 years after Christ's Resurrection. There was no time during those 1900 years a prediction like that had any earthly potential. No military in the world - no parasite or virus - has ever had the power to destroy all flesh, until now. Since the 1950s, the world powers have produced enough nuclear warheads to wipe out all life on the planet - maybe even the cockroaches.

Jeremiah 50 describes the yet-future final destruction of Babylon on the Day of the LORD, and verse 50:9 describes smart weapons. The wording places the skill in the arrows themselves, and not the shooter; "none shall return in vain." We can now program missiles to hit, not just buildings, but specific windows in buildings while sitting at computers thousands of miles away.

Jesus describes something very strange in Matthew 24. He warns His followers in Judea to escape to the mountains when they see the Abomination that Causes Desolation in the Holy Place. Yet, these people do not have to be in the Temple itself to see the Abomination:

> *When ye therefore shall see the abomination of desolation, spoken of by Daniel the prophet, stand in the holy place, (whoso readeth, let him understand:) Then let them which be in Judaea flee into the mountains: Let him which is on the housetop not come down to take any thing out of his house:*

> *Neither let him which is in the field return back to take his clothes.*
>
> Matthew 24:15-18

Have you ever read this passage and wondered how exactly they were supposed to see something going on inside the Temple while they were standing on rooftops or working out in the field? Never in history was this possible - until now. Here in the 21st century, even children customarily carry around a small computer with access to all the world's news. These handy devices fit comfortably in our pockets, and we use them to communicate with people anywhere in the world. We can take pictures and video, and in minutes or seconds we can post them on the Internet for anybody to see. It is now possible for people on rooftops to see the Antichrist take his seat in the Holy of Holies pretending to be God.[8]

Revelation 13:17 describes a time when nobody will be able to buy or sell without the Mark of the Beast. A mark designating loyalty - a tattoo or a brand - could certainly have been used before now. However, the global aspect of this prophecy is certainly much simpler now than ever before. Technology makes it easy to never carry cash. Our funds are all digital, which those with a 401K know far too well. People have lost their life savings in a day when the markets crashed. It's simple to freeze accounts or to block a card number. Whether the Mark of the Beast is a tattoo or a computer chip or a code number, the technology in our current global economy makes it very possible to block people from buying or selling - wherever they are in the world.

The Bible does not systematically spell out natural history for scientists. However, modern science has finally caught up to the Bible and has confirmed the truth of many of its statements.

King David mentioned the "paths of the seas" in Psalm 8:8. The 19th century scientist Matthew Fontaine Maury is known as the Father of Modern Oceanography, and he was one of the driving forces behind a national naval observatory. He is also nicknamed the "Pathfinder of the Seas" because he devoted his life to finding these paths of the seas mentioned by David. After years dedicated to studying old ship logs and charts to determine the ocean currents, in 1847 he published the "Wind and Current Chart of the North Atlantic."

In Job we find descriptions of the water cycle.[9] In Leviticus, God ordered the Israelites to let the land rest every seventh year,[10] which we now know is important for preserving the health of the soil. It's well known that Moses's descriptions of medical treatment and hygiene were far superior to the Egyptian practices of his time. We could spend chapters on just the medical wisdom contained in Leviticus. In a time when they did not understand about genetics, Moses forbade the marriage of close family members.[11] In a time when they did not understand about bacteria, the Law gave instructions that protected the Israelites from catching and spreading infection.[12] We take for granted that the Scriptures give practical medical wisdom that anticipates modern microbiology. The Bible looks ahead to technological advances thousands of years in advance.

Unlike any other religious book, the Bible freely recognizes the existence of additional dimensions. It wasn't until the 20th century that physicists finally had the mathematical sophistication to recognize and describe them.[13] The invisible angelic world revealed in 2 Kings 6 and Daniel 10 suggests more than four space-time dimensions, but there are other hints as well. We can take a different approach to mysteries like the spinning "wheels" of Ezekiel 1 and 10 when we understand that Ezekiel was trying to describe objects in a realm of more than four dimensions. In Luke 24:13-43, Jesus was able to disappear from Emmaus and appear to the disciples after the Resurrection without walking through a door. This argues that Jesus in His resurrected form enjoyed a greater dimensionality than we do.

Beyond Time and Space

Our God is the God outside of time. He sees the end from the beginning. He *is* the beginning and the end.[14] We discover that the Bible is not just a collection of Hebrew law and history, but one single story written by a master Storyteller. From the serpent in the Garden to the final demise of Satan in Revelation 20, we find the great work of God to save fallen humanity. What's more, He tells us His purposes from the very beginning, giving us His plan through prophecies and prophetic types.

As we read the Bible, we need to remember that we have God's own words in our hands. These are not opinions about God or speculations. The original Hebrew words were God-breathed. He describes events centuries before they take place.

- In Isaiah 44:28-45:6, God names Cyrus, the future King of Persia who would send the exiled Jews in Babylon home to rebuild the Temple. He did this 100 years before Cyrus the Great was even born.
- In Daniel 9:24-26, Gabriel explains that Jerusalem would be rebuilt during difficult times, and the city and Temple would be destroyed yet again. Gabriel gave this prophecy 600 years before the Romans came in and wiped out the Jews in A.D. 70. If we do the math on Gabriel's prophecy of 69 weeks in this same passage, it brings us to the exact day that Jesus rode a donkey into town on Palm Sunday in fulfillment of Zechariah 9:9.[15]

Most importantly, the person of Jesus Christ can be found on every page. The details of Jesus' life were written in advance millennia before He was born. We find Him suffering on the cross in Psalm 22. We find an explanation for His painful sacrifice in Isaiah 53. Jesus was crucified on Passover as our Passover Lamb, whose blood covers us and protects us from spiritual death. He is the scapegoat and the sacrifice on Yom Kippur, the Day of Atonement. He is the Son of David, the coming Messiah whose beautiful reign is described in Isaiah 11. Jesus Christ fulfills hundreds of specific prophecies written long before His birth in a stable in Bethlehem.

> *But thou, Bethlehem Ephratah, though thou be little among the thousands of Judah, yet out of thee shall he come forth unto me that is to be ruler in Israel; whose goings forth have been from of old, from everlasting.*
>
> Micah 5:2

Once we understand who Jesus Christ is, we realize that He is able to authenticate the whole package. There are two principle discoveries I have made in studying the Bible. The first is that these 66 books were penned by more than 40 different authors over thousands of years, yet these books are clearly an integrated message. The second is that the Bible originated from outside the "time" domain. There is an integrity of design in the Bible from Genesis to Revelation, and it had to have a supernatural origin with one ultimate Author.

Prophetic "Types"

I'm not just referring to out-right prophecy. There are times the Bible includes isolated events that are puzzling until they are explained later in the Bible. God gives us His plan in bits and pieces, using similes and metaphors in the form of object lessons. He warned us He would communicate to us this way:

> *I have also spoken by the prophets, and I have multiplied visions, and used similitudes, by the ministry of the prophets.*
>
> Hosea 12:10

> *For precept must be upon precept, precept upon precept; line upon line, line upon line; here a little, and there a little:*
>
> Isaiah 28:10

For example, in Numbers 21, the Israelites are bitten by poisonous snakes and are dying. God instructs Moses to make a bronze serpent on a pole, telling him in verse eight, "*every one that is bitten, when he looketh upon it, shall live.*"

It's a strange story. The fiery snakes bit the Israelites and caused them to die, so it seems strange God would have Moses put a bronze snake (yet another fiery serpent) on a pole. "Look to the snake and be healed?" What! That just doesn't jive. Yet, the serpent symbolism continued to be handed down through history. A thousand years later, it leaked into the myth of Asclepius, a Greek god of healing and medicine who carried a rod with a snake wrapped around it. We still see this symbol in the medical field today.

A serpent on a pole makes no sense as a symbol of healing. In the Bible, the serpent consistently represents evil. No explanation is given in the Old Testament for the bronze snake. A full 1500 years after the incident in the desert, Jesus finally explains the snake symbolism in His midnight meeting with Nicodemus:

> *And as Moses lifted up the serpent in the wilderness, even so must the Son of man be lifted up: That whosoever believeth in him should not perish, but have eternal life.*
>
> John 3:14-15

With those few words, the bronze serpent suddenly makes sense. The reason it's a serpent on the pole, a symbol of evil, is that Jesus became sin for us[16] - and when we look to Him, we are healed.

Macro Codes

There are dozens of these. In the computer field, we call them "macro codes" - a set of codes that anticipates data in advance. For instance, in Word we can push a button that automatically creates a Table of Contents from the chapter titles of a document. We can push another button to put all the footnotes at the end of the document. In other words, we can tell the computer what to do in terms of structure with codes set up in advance.

The Bible uses macro codes. Throughout the Old Testament, we find "types." These are people or laws or feast days or cities - that foreshadow a greater reality in the future. They may or may not make sense in themselves. When the things they typify are fulfilled, we find the picture they foreshadow is astonishingly precise. Consider the story of Isaac:

> *And he said, Take now thy son, thine only son Isaac, whom thou lovest, and get thee into the land of Moriah; and offer him there for a burnt offering upon one of the mountains which I will tell thee of.*
>
> Genesis 22:2

Abraham is told to offer his son on a particular spot on planet Earth, the mountains of Moriah. Moriah literally means, "Seen of the LORD." God had promised Abraham in Gen 17:19 that He would establish an everlasting covenant with Isaac and Isaac's seed, yet here God instructs Abraham to go offer Isaac as burnt offering. Abraham proceeds to obey God, trusting God to keep His promise. Hebrews 11:17-19 tells us that Abraham believed that God was able to raise Isaac from the dead if necessary. Abraham therefore went to a mountain in the land of Moriah to sacrifice his son - the son God had promised him. We know the story. God stopped Abraham from killing Isaac and provided a ram in place of the young man.

God used this event to test Abraham's dedication and faith, but He used it for something even more important. That picture of a father sacrificing his son on Mount Moriah was fulfilled 2100 years later when God sacrificed His only Son for us. In fact, Mount Moriah is a hill in Jerusalem, and it may be that Jesus was sacrificed on the same hilltop where God prevented Abraham from sacrificing Isaac. God chose that mountain for Abraham, after all. What's more, Abraham knew the event was prophetic, because he named the place *Jehovah Jireh* - "Yahweh sees" - creating the saying, "In the mount of the LORD it shall be seen."[17]

God provided that picture for us thousands of years in advance. Just as Abraham anticipated what God would do for Isaac, God did for His own sacrificed Son when He raised Him from the dead.

The bronze serpent on the pole and the "sacrifice" of Isaac are just two types that are fulfilled by Jesus Christ. Prophetic types abound in the Old Testament.

- Moses represented the Law, but he wasn't able to enter the Promised Land. We don't get to Heaven by the Law, but by grace through Jesus Christ. Jesus is the Greek form of "Joshua" - and it was Joshua, not Moses, who led the people into the Promised Land.
- David was the despised shepherd boy who trusted in God, slew the giant, and became the king. Jesus is our shepherd. He was despised, yet He has conquered death, and He will return one day to sit

on the throne of David and become the eternal King.

- Boaz was the kinsman redeemer who married Ruth, a Gentile bride, who met him through Naomi, the Jewish mother. The Church is the Bride of Christ, whom she met through mother Israel. Christ is our kinsman, born of Adam, and He has redeemed us from our debt and given us back the inheritance we lost. The Old Testament is filled with these.

The types and prophecies we find throughout the Old Testament and fulfilled in the New Testament demonstrate that the Bible is an integrated message system written by one Author. You and I are beneficiaries of Albert Einstein's insights that *time is a physical property*. We know today that time is a dimension that can stretch or shorten with mass, acceleration, and gravity. God is not subject to mass or acceleration or gravity. God is not Somebody with a lot of time; He is outside the time dimension altogether. He uses that attribute to authenticate His message by describing things before they happen.

We should not try to use the Bible to tell the future. The Bible is not an instrument of divination, and we can't use it to set dates or make specific predictions for our personal benefit. We can glean general ideas like, "Don't take the Mark of the Beast" or "Jesus is going to return." We can anticipate that a third Temple will be built. The Bible is clear about those things. But it's not a future-telling device. At the same time, the prophecies in the Bible *can* be used to authenticate the message we have in our hands.

It's interesting that the Old Testament is an incomplete book. It contains a multitude of prophecies that were not fulfilled in the days of its prophets. The Old Testament needs the New Testament to see the accomplishment of the promises God made to the Hebrews. Jesus fulfilled a multitude of prophecies during His first appearance, and He will fulfill a multitude more when He returns to reign on the throne of David in Jerusalem. We see in Revelation the completion of every promise - including Old Testament prophecies with end dates still in our future.

We find something else interesting about the Old Testament; it includes a number of unappeased longings. God longs to fulfill His Word. It is only His patient longsuffering and His desire for more people to be saved that He holds off the final act of the cosmic drama.[18] We find in the poetical books and the prophets this aching heart of God. Even when God promises judgment and punishment against His disobedient and unrepentant people, He constantly returns His focus to a future day when He will be able to gather His children and enjoy them:

> *The LORD thy God in the midst of thee is mighty; he will save, he will rejoice over*

thee with joy; he will rest in his love, he will joy over thee with singing... At that time will I bring you again, even in the time that I gather you: for I will make you a name and a praise among all people of the earth, when I turn back your captivity before your eyes, saith the LORD.

Zephaniah 3:17, 20

Chapter 3
Getting to the Nitty Gritty

As we enter into studying the Bible, it's vital to understand that we're not dealing with something so simple as Jewish history and cultural mores. We are actually dealing with God's own words. It is true that each ancient author had his own writing style and favorite vocabulary - each one had a specific focus and approach. Yet, we also find God's fingerprints involved in the very wording they used. We constantly read, "*The word of the LORD came to*" this or that prophet. Paul told Timothy, "*All scripture is given by inspiration of God...*"[19] The Greek word for "inspiration" here literally means, "breathed into." There is far more to the Bible than the opinionated jottings of long-dead Hebrew sages.

That doesn't mean that copyist errors and translation confusion haven't crept in. We find places where somebody wrote the wrong number or left out a line. Even then, the Hebrew copyists through the ages have been so dedicated in transmitting the words of God, they wouldn't "correct" mistakes when they thought they found them. They just made notes in the margins. These little errors are few and far between, and they do nothing to change any major doctrines of the Bible.

We trust that the original autographs by the original writers were created through the inspiration of God. Computers have allowed us to demonstrate that God had to have given the prophets their messages word by word. There are properties to the text that disappear if we change even one letter.

With this in mind, how do we begin our study of the Bible?

Openness to the Truth

First, it's important that we approach our Bible study with a mind ready to receive the truth. Remember, there is one certain barrier to discovering the truth, and that's the conviction that you already have it. As librarian of the U.S. Congress Daniel J. Boorstin famously said: "The greatest obstacle to discovery is not ignorance - it is the illusion of knowledge."[20] It may be that we already know quite a bit about the subject we are studying, but it may also be we've picked up misunderstandings in our lives. We need to be open to the Holy Spirit as we approach the Word of God, to hear what He has to say and to catch a full view of the insights He wants to show us.

God is not afraid of our questions. It doesn't worry Him when we are puzzled. He does not frown when we boldly dig deeper to figure out what is really going on. God wants us to know the truth, and the Bible constantly praises those who diligently search out answers. I constantly remind my students of Luke's admiration for the noble Bereans in Acts 17:11, because they were willing to hear what Paul had to say, but they also dug into the Scriptures to make sure Paul was on the right track. That's appropriate behavior. The Bereans had the same heart that was encouraged by Solomon:

> *Yea, if thou criest after knowledge, and liftest up thy voice for understanding; If thou seekest her as silver, and searchest for her as for hid treasures; Then shalt thou understand the fear of the LORD, and find the knowledge of God. For the LORD giveth wisdom: out of his mouth cometh knowledge and understanding.*
>
> Proverbs 2:3-6

Seeking Knowledge

There are certain fields of study that deal with the correct way to approach knowledge and interpreting the Bible. We recognize that pulling open the Bible and pointing at a line is not a good way to get messages from God. You could come across a very unfortunate order of verses:

> *And he cast down the pieces of silver in the temple, and departed, and went and hanged himself.*
>
> Matthew 27:5

Then said Jesus unto him, Go, and do thou likewise.

Luke 10:37b

The open-and-point method is an unwise strategy of Bible study. I do not recommend it. There are entire disciplines dedicated to wisdom in seeking knowledge about the Bible. Let's look at the major ones.

- ***Epistemology*** is the study of knowledge, its scope and limits. It's the discipline which governs how we discern between actual knowledge and mere opinion.
- ***Exegesis*** is the careful interpretation and explanation of the Scriptures, and it often requires the study of the original Hebrew and Greek. The word *exegesis* comes from the Greek and means, "to lead out of." Thus, true exegesis always draws information from the text itself, as opposed to *eisegesis*, in which a person reads into the text whatever they already have in their own head. Exegesis does justice to the original meaning of the text, and eisegesis does not. People who employ eisegesis generally twist the text to further their own agendas.
- ***Exposition*** is the explanation of the Scriptures. After we know what a passage says through exegesis, we have to figure out what it means and how it applies to us. Teachers of the Bible engage in

exposition when they interpret the purpose and intention of passages and help students understand them.

- ***Hermeneutics*** is the field of study dedicated to biblical interpretation. Good hermeneutics follows specific principles - like using exegesis and not eisegesis. When we use solid hermeneutics, we come to a completely different place than those who simply allegorize certain passages from their own imaginations.
- ***Homiletics*** is the discipline of writing and delivering sermons or teachings about the Scriptures.

Pilate famous asked Jesus a rhetorical question, "What is truth?" We find a relativism in our universities today. It's hard to find professors who teach that truth exists. Yet the Lord commanded us, "*Be not deceived.*"[21] If we can be deceived, that means that there is an objective truth. If there's no truth, there can be no deception, because every man's idea is as good as every other man's. How do we figure out what is true? We make use of the tools in the disciplines of epistemology and hermeneutics.

People like to say, "You can't prove the Bible is true." I disagree. I've been researching the Bible for fifty or sixty years. It's possible to demonstrate that the Bible is not just true, but is covered with God's fingerprints.

Hebrew Hermeneutics

Hebrew hermeneutics is a little different than Christian hermeneutics. Christians see three levels of meaning in every text. First, there's the direct, literal meaning. Then, there's the deeper meaning behind the literal meaning. Finally, there's the practical application.

For instance, in Isaiah 7, Isaiah gives Judah's King Ahaz a prophecy that has since become famous. Isaiah declares that a young woman would give birth, and before the child was able to tell right from wrong, the kings of Samaria and Damascus would fall. The child's name would be *Immanuel*, "God with us," representing God's presence in the situation in Isaiah's day. The immediate, literal meaning of the passage involves a young woman who gave birth to a child within a year or so after Isaiah's prophecy. If we look deeper, however, we discover that this is also a prophecy of the Messiah. In its greater fulfillment, an actual virgin gave birth, and the child Immanuel was Jesus Christ, who is literally "God with us." A practical application of the passage is to learn the lesson that Ahaz should have learned; to trust God completely.

We see here in Isaiah 7 the literal meaning, the deeper prophetic meaning (which Matthew explains to us in Matthew 1:22-23, so that we don't miss it), and a practical application.

Hebrew hermeneutics includes these three but also adds a fourth level of meaning.

1) *Pashat* refers to the literal or direct meaning of the Word of God.
2) *Remez* refers to the hint of something deeper.
3) *Drash* is the homiletic or practical approach to Bible study.
4) *Sod* is the additional level - the *hidden* or mystical meaning that complements the *Remez.*

In Christian hermeneutics, we recognize that there might be a deeper or allegorical meaning beyond the literal, immediate meaning of a passage, but the Jews go even further and suggest that there is a hidden meaning in the passages. There's a mnemonic they use to remember these four levels: PaRDeS, or Pardes. In Hebrew, the word *pardes* means "orchard" and our word "paradise" comes from the same Iranian root word.

We have to be careful when we approach Bible study not to ignore the literal and direct meaning and only go hunting for the deeper or hidden meaning. What's more, we can't just invent "deeper" or "hidden" meanings for the fun of it. In all our study, our goal is to find what God actually intended to communicate in each passage. In Isaiah 7, God intended to communicate to Ahaz that he needed to trust the LORD. God intended to include a prophesy of the Messiah's virgin birth. There is no place for us to just make things up as we like, putting into the Scriptures our own ideas, or making the Scriptures justify us and what we want to do. Our goal is always to find the treasures that God purposely placed there.

Sod

When we consider the *Sod*, the hidden or mystical meaning of a passage, we don't find hidden knowledge that is not in the plain text of the Bible. We often just find fun little tidbits we didn't expect were there, tidbits that complement the doctrines God has made clear in the plain text. Sometimes they are truths hidden in the Old Testament and revealed in the New. Consider the first few verses of Proverbs 30:

In Proverbs 30:1 we find an odd list of names - people we don't hear of elsewhere. We cannot find out anything about these people. Bible dictionaries can't tell us who they are:

> *The words of Agur the son of Jakeh, even the prophecy: the man spake unto Ithiel, even unto Ithiel and Ucal...*

We have to remember that we are reading a translation of the Bible. The King James translators listed four names in this verse: Agur, Jakeh, Ithiel, Ucal. When we look at their original meanings, however, we find that these names are better translated as titles.

Agur:	The Collector
Jakeh:	Carefully Religious.
	The Pious One

Ithiel:	God has arrived
Ucal:	To be consumed

The book of Proverbs contains just a portion of the 3000 proverbs that 1 Kings 4:32 tells us Solomon wrote (along with 1005 songs). Many commentators suggest that *Agur*, the "Collector" or the "Receiver" is just a title for Solomon. The Book of Ecclesiastes was also written by Solomon, who titles himself *Qoheleth*, the Preacher at its beginning.

In Proverbs 30:1, we find Agur "The Collector" is the son of Jakeh, which means, "The Pious One." We have a mysterious collector of wise sayings. This was something that Solomon liked to traffic in. He's known as the collector or dealer in riddles. In Proverbs 1:6, he notes that he collects wisdom, "*to understand a proverb, and the interpretation; the words of the wise, and their dark sayings.*" He is interested in enigmas and hidden meanings. His father, David, was a man after God's own heart, who wrote psalms like Psalm 119 - which praises the blessings of the Law. We therefore have The Collector, the son of the Pious One.

By the way, 2 Samuel 12:24-25 tells us that Solomon had two names. Solomon was his royal name, but he was also called Jedidiah, which means, "loved by Yaweh." This was the name God gave Solomon at his birth through Nathan the prophet. His public name was Solomon, which means "peaceful," and the land was at peace during his reign. His private name, though, was Jedidiah, "loved by Yahweh" - God's name for him. This is interesting, because David also means, "beloved" and Jedidiah was David's son.

We also find out in Proverbs 30:1 that this is a prophecy. The word translated "man" is actually "warrior" or "mighty" and the word "spake" can also be translated "oracle." Thus we could retranslate Proverbs 30:1 to say, "The words collected by the son of the pious one, even the prophecy, the mighty oracle unto God arrives to be consumed."

What does that mean?

In John 6:33, Jesus says:

For the bread of God is he which cometh down from heaven, and giveth life unto the world.

He goes on to say in verse 6:51:

I am the living bread which came down from heaven: if any man eat of this bread, he shall live for ever: and the bread that I will give is my flesh, which I will give for the life of the world.

Jesus' language gets even more shocking. Of course, we know that Jesus is *not* promoting cannibalism. He isn't talking about physical things. He's distinguishing physical bread from the spiritual bread that He offers us - and the spiritual is far more important. Those who ate the manna in the wilderness all died, but he who eats of the spiritual bread Jesus offers - His sacrifice of Himself - will never die.

We then find reference to Christ's ascent and descent in Proverbs 30 here.

> *Who hath ascended up into heaven, or descended? who hath gathered the wind in his fists? who hath bound the waters in a garment? who hath established all the ends of the earth? what is his name, and what is his son's name, if thou canst tell?*
>
> Proverbs 30:4

When we read these questions, we think we're in Job 38, when God demands answers from Job and gives him a science quiz.

Who ascended up to heaven? That's Hosea 5:15 - "*I will go and return to my place, till they acknowledge their offence...*"

Who gathered the wind in His fists? That's Psalm 135:7 - "*... he bringeth the wind out of his treasuries.*"

Who established the ends of the earth? That's Psalm 72:8: "*He shall have dominion also from sea to sea, and from the river unto the ends of the earth.*"

What is His name and what is His Son's name? That's Psalm 110:1 - "*The LORD said unto my Lord, Sit thou at my right hand, until I make thine enemies thy footstool.*"

Jesus uses this last verse to confound the Pharisees in Matthew 22:41-46:

He saith unto them, How then doth David in spirit call him Lord, saying, The LORD said unto my Lord, Sit thou on my right hand, till I make thine enemies thy footstool? If David then call him Lord, how is he his son? And no man was able to answer him a word, neither durst any man from that day forth ask him any more questions.

Matthew 22:43-46

I love it. He shut them up.

The point is that we find this little treasure in Proverbs 30 if we do a little digging. We know that Jesus ascended, and we know that one day He will descend again. He is the God who arrived to be consumed. He is the Bread of Life. We have a small prophecy here in Proverbs regarding the Messiah as the Son of God. It doesn't change our doctrine or our views of God. It's just a fun hidden treasure that reminds us of God's fingerprints all over the Old Testament.

Every word of God is pure: he is a shield unto them that put their trust in him. Add thou not unto his words, lest he reprove thee, and thou be found a liar.

Proverbs 30:5-6

Rhetorical Devices:

There are many different figures of speech in the Scripture. When people say, "I take the Bible literally," a variety of skeptics instantly appear to quibble. They might fuss over whether God has feathers, because Psalm 91:4 says, "*He shall cover thee with his feathers, and under his wings shalt thou trust...*" Of course, they're being silly, because descriptives like this are rhetorical devices and are not meant to be taken literally. The Bible uses a large number of literary tools to create pictures and develop understanding in our minds.

Simile uses "like" or "as" to compare two things:

- Psalm 77:20 - "*Thou leddest thy people like a flock...*"
- Songs 4:2 - "*Thy teeth are like a flock of sheep...*"

Metaphor compares two things directly without using *like* or *as*:

- Ezekiel 34:31 - "*Ye [are] my flock...*"
- Psalm 23:1 - "*The LORD is my shepherd...*"

Hypocatastasis implies the person or thing that is being compared without saying it directly:

- Ezekiel 34:8 - "*...but the shepherds fed themselves, and fed not my flock...*"
- Jeremiah 23:3 - "*And I will gather the remnant of my flock...*"

Synecdoche uses a part to represent the whole. When we say, "head of cattle" we do not mean only the cow heads. We mean the entire beast, but we count them by counting their heads. We can use a *part* to represent the whole.

- Leviticus 19:32 - "*Thou shalt rise up before the hoary head...*"
- Isaiah 54:17 - "*...every tongue that shall rise against thee in judgment thou shalt condemn...*"

Metonymy refers to things by items associated with them - calling businessmen "suits," for instance.

- Leviticus 26:6 - "*...neither shall the sword go through your land.*"
- Luke 1:69 - "*And hath raised up an horn of salvation for us in the house of his servant David;*"

The Bible uses alliteration and acrostics, parallelism and paradox. There are a multitude of different kinds of rhetorical devices in the Scripture. Paul gives us a clue in 1 Corinthians 10 when he's talking about the history of Israel, saying:

> *Now all these things happened unto them for ensamples: and they are written for our admonition, upon whom the ends of the world are come.*
>
> 1 Corinthians 10:11

Chapter 4
Jesus and Prophecy

We think of prophecy as prediction and fulfillment. The Hebrew model is a little different. The ancient Hebrews saw prophecy as a *pattern*, which is why types become so significant.

We find that Bible prophecy can be multifaceted, and some prophesies are fulfilled more than once. For instance, while John the Baptist came like Elijah, we believe that the actual Elijah will precede Christ's Second Coming. The types and prophecies are everywhere, and there are additional prophecies clearly awaiting fulfillment.

We look through the Old Testament and find quaint rules and strange resolutions to problems, but Paul lets us know that they were examples. I've used the word "type" in this book, but a word more familiar to us would be "model." The Bible uses models as examples for us.

The sacrifice on the brazen altar is a type of the cross. Jesus Himself explained that He is the Bread of Life - represented by the manna in the desert.[22] Paul tells us Jesus was the rock in the desert that Moses struck so that water came out.[23] Jesus offers living water.[24] Jesus is the scape goat on Yom Kippur. He was crucified on Passover as the ultimate fulfillment of the night the Angel of the Lord passed over the Israelites. When John the Baptist introduced Jesus Christ publicly for the first time, he said, "*Behold the Lamb of God, which taketh away the sin of the world.*"[25]

Each one of these are models. Each one of these types point to Jesus Christ.

We find a wide range of metaphors used to describe Jesus Christ. He is the "Lion of the tribe of Judah" in Revelation 5:5, hearkening back to Jacob's blessing on Judah in Genesis 49:8-10. Jesus is the Lily of the valleys in Songs 2:1 and the Root out of dry ground in Isaiah 11:10 and 53:2. He is the Righteous Branch,[26] and the Rejected Cornerstone.[27] In all these metaphors, we see that Jesus Christ is like a hologram. In the natural light, He has no comeliness that we might desire Him,[28] but illuminated by the Holy Spirit, He's altogether lovely.[29]

The Old Testament is the study of a nation. The New Testament is the story of a man.

The Old Testament contains thousands of prophecies. We find that a large number are specifically noted as fulfilled by Jesus in the New Testament. The following table contains just a few examples:

Quality / Action	Old Testament Prophecies	New Testament Fulfillment
The Son/ Descendant of David	2 Sam 7:12-16; Psalm 89:3-4; Psalm 132:11; Isaiah 9:7; Isaiah 11:1	Mat 1:20; Luke 1:30-33; Mark 10:47-52
Greater than David	Psalm 110:1; Isaiah 9:6	Mat 22:42-45; Eph 1:20-21
Born of a Virgin	Genesis 3:15; Isaiah 7:14	Mat 1:18-23; Luke 1:30-35
Born in Bethlehem	Micah 5:2	Mat 2:1-6; Luke 2:4-7
Sojourner in Egypt	Hosea 11:1	Mat 2:13-15
From Galilee	Isaiah 9:1-2	Luke 2:39; Mark 1:9
Announced by a Herald	Isaiah 40:3; Mal 3:1	Mat 3:1-3; Mark 1:2-5; John 1:21-29
Preceded by Elijah	Mal 4:5; 2 Kings 1:8	Mat 3:4; 11:13-14; Mark 1:6
A Light to the Gentiles	Isaiah 11:10; 42:6-7; 49:6	Mat 8:5-13; Luke 2:32; Luke 17:15-19
A Healer/ Rescuer	Isaiah 35:2-5; 42:7; 53:5; 61:1	Luke 4:17-21; 7:22
Rejected by His Own	Psalm 69:4; 118:22; Isaiah 53:3	Mark 12:10-12; Luke 9:22; John 1:11
Presented on Donkey	Zec 9:9	John 12:12-16
Betrayed for 30 Pieces of Silver	Zec 11:12-13	Mat 26:14-16; 27:3-10
His Sheep Scattered	Zec 13:7	Mat 26:31; Mark 14:50-52
Given Gall to Drink	Psalm 69:21	Mat 27:34
They Cast Lots for His Clothes	Psalm 22:18	Mat 27:35; John 19:23-24
Pierced	Psalm 22:16; Zec 12:10	Mat 27:26; John 20:26-28

Quality / Action	Old Testament Prophecies	New Testament Fulfillment
Silent like a Lamb	Isaiah 53:7	Mat 26:62-63; Luke 23:8-9
Sacrificed for Sin	Isaiah 53:6,10,11	John 1:29; 3:16; 1 John 2:2
Would Rise from Dead	Psalm 16:10; Isaiah 53:12	Luke 24:3-8; Acts 2:29-31

Here we see just 20 examples of the prophecies that Jesus fulfilled, and these are just the tip of the proverbial iceberg. He is found from Genesis to Malachi in all manner of images and models that foreshadow His eternal work and purpose. We don't find these prophecies spelled out as a straight forward list. They are found here and there, woven into the Scriptures.

Ancient Testimonies

In volume 18 of Josephus' work *The Antiquities of the Jews*, we find this little section:

> Now there was about this time Jesus, a wise man, if it be lawful to call him a man; for he was a doer of wonderful works, a teacher of such men as receive the truth with pleasure. He drew over to him both many of the Jews and many of the Gentiles. He was [the] Christ. And when Pilate, at the suggestion of the principle men among us, had condemned him to the cross, those that loved him at the first did not forsake him; for he appeared to them alive again the third day; as the divine prophets had foretold these and ten thousand

> other wonderful things concerning him. And the tribe of Christians, so named from him, are not extinct at this day.[30]

Whether this was originally written by Josephus or not is a matter of debate, but it again points to the view among the early Christians that Jesus came according to the Scriptures - "as the divine prophets had foretold..."

When we go back and look at the Old Testament, we realize it was all laid out in advance. If Jesus was doing a marketing job, it was a lousy one. It got Him crucified, and He did nothing to stop it. The First Commandment, the bedrock of the Law, declared that there is only one God. Yet, Jesus absolutely claimed to be God. That's why they killed him. Anyone that says that Jesus didn't claim to be God hasn't read the Gospel of John.

We also have the witness of the disciples' lives. The followers of Christ not only claimed to have seen Him after His death, but they went to their own deaths for the truth they proclaimed. Even when they had nothing to gain but torture and imprisonment and execution, they insisted that Jesus died and rose again according to the Scriptures. From Peter and James to Thomas, not one yielded or bent or caved in. Peter was executed upside down on a cross.[31] James was killed with the sword.[32] Thomas preached the Gospel in India, where he was speared to death.[33]

More than a Rabbi

Nice teachings and wonderful ideas cannot rescue a person from a burning building. The crucifixion was not a tragedy. It was an achievement. Jesus agreed to it before the universe began. The entire panorama of God's redemption was built in advance on the cross.

Many people will say that Jesus was a great teacher - and indeed He was a great teacher. Yet, limiting Him to that simple role misses the point, because wonderful ideas don't rescue us from a burning building. The incarnation of Jesus Christ divides Him from other political, religious, and social leaders. He didn't just consider Himself a good teacher, but the very Son of God and the Creator of the world. Jesus said ridiculous things that would be reprehensible for any mere human to say. He could say them, however, because He was far more than just a rabbi.

Jesus claimed to be the Bread of Life in John 6:35, saying:

> *I am the bread of life: he that cometh to me shall never hunger; and he that believeth on me shall never thirst.*

Vladimir Lenin promised bread in every household under Communism. It didn't work out well, but that's what he promised. Even in his greatest hubris, Lenin never claimed to be the Bread of Life.

Jesus claimed to be the Light of the World in John 8:12, saying:

> *I am the light of the world: he that followeth me shall not walk in darkness, but shall have the light of life.*

Jesus also told his followers they were the light of the world in Matthew 5:14, clearly because those that follow him will not walk in darkness but will have the light of life! On the other hand, Buddha taught enlightenment, but he never had the audacity to say that he himself was that light.

Jesus claimed to be the source of true peace in John 14:27, saying:

> *Peace I leave with you, my peace I give unto you: not as the world giveth, give I unto you. Let not your heart be troubled, neither let it be afraid.*

Sigmund Freud used psychotherapy in his efforts to heal emotional and spiritual pain. He never once suggested that he was the source of peace.

If ever we miss Jesus' claims to be God, the Pharisees come to our rescue by wanting to stone Him. Remember when He said He was before Abraham?

> *Your father Abraham rejoiced to see my day: and he saw it, and was glad. Then said the Jews unto him, Thou art*

> *not yet fifty years old, and hast thou seen Abraham? Jesus said unto them, Verily, verily, I say unto you, Before Abraham was, I am. Then took they up stones to cast at him: but Jesus hid himself, and went out of the temple, going through the midst of them, and so passed by.*
>
> John 8:56-59

Jesus uses a particularly bold phrase here. He says, "*Before Abraham was, I AM,*" which is point-blank referring to Himself as the voice of the Burning Bush in Exodus 3:14. There God tells Moses, "*Thus shalt thou say unto the children of Israel, I AM hath sent me unto you.*" This infuriates the Pharisees, and they all grab rocks to stone Jesus, but He just passes through them and leaves.

Jesus constantly proclaimed himself to be Somebody much greater than any human teacher.

> *And I give unto them eternal life; and they shall never perish, neither shall any man pluck them out of my hand. My Father, which gave them me, is greater than all; and no man is able to pluck them out of my Father's hand. I and my Father are one. Then the Jews took up stones again to stone him.*
>
> John 10:28-31

They never do succeed in stoning Him. Notice here that Jesus not only claims to be one with the

Father, but He has the temerity to claim that He gives His sheep eternal life. If there's any question about what it means to be one with the Father, there is no question that mere humans have no power to save themselves, let alone to offer others eternal life. This is not something a human can give - unless He is also God Himself.

Many religious men have been martyred over the millennia. Jesus Christ validated His identity by rising again from the dead. His death is well-documented, but His Resurrection is documented even better. Only people who have died were able to witness His crucifixion, but there are multitudes of people today still experiencing the power of His Resurrection and His work in their lives.

Jesus had to be God, because He had to be able to present Himself as the pure, spotless Lamb. The Bible explains to us that Jesus' sacrifice was not an afterthought; it was all God's plan from the beginning of the world.

> *Then shall the King say unto them on his right hand, Come, ye blessed of my Father, inherit the kingdom prepared for you from the foundation of the world:*
>
> Matthew 25:34

> *For we which have believed do enter into rest, as he said, As I have sworn in my wrath, if they shall enter into my rest:*

> *although the works were finished from the foundation of the world.*
>
> Hebrews 4:3

> *Who verily was foreordained before the foundation of the world, but was manifest in these last times for you,*
>
> 1 Peter 1:20

> *And all that dwell upon the earth shall worship him, whose names are not written in the book of life of the Lamb slain from the foundation of the world.*
>
> Revelation 13:8

Many people believe that there are many paths to God. If there are many paths to God, then Jesus' prayers were not answered. In agony in the Garden of Gethsemane, Jesus prayed, "*O my Father, if it be possible, let this cup pass from me: nevertheless not as I will, but as thou wilt.*"[34] His prayers were so intense, Luke the doctor tells us that He sweated blood.[35] Three times He prayed earnestly to be taken off the hook, but even in His torment, Jesus agreed, "Thy will be done." If there was any way to get to God other than through the cross, then Jesus Christ's prayer was not answered.

We don't understand how bad sin is, and we tend to compare ourselves with the guy next to us. That's not the real problem, though. Our real problem is that we don't understand God's holiness. Once we start to understand holiness, we realize how impossible it is to cross that gulf by our own power. Only God can meet His own requirements, and He did just that through Jesus Christ. Christianity stands in unbending opposition to any notion that salvation is the result of our own efforts. Our attempts to add to what God has completed is a form of blasphemy.

Chapter 5
The Great Adventure

We see a vacuous Christianity across our landscape. We see a God without wrath, who would bring human beings into a kingdom without judgment, through the ministry of a Christ without a cross. The truth is not about what is nice or pretty. We need to be about the truth, even when it's hard to hear.

Jesus warned about false teachers. Jude describes them:

> *Woe unto them! for they have gone in the way of Cain, and ran greedily after the error of Balaam for reward, and perished in the gainsaying of Core. These are spots in your feasts of charity, when they feast with you, feeding themselves without fear: clouds they are without water, carried about of winds; trees whose fruit withereth, without fruit, twice dead, plucked up by the roots; Raging waves of the sea, foaming out their own shame; wandering stars, to whom is reserved the blackness of darkness forever.*
>
> Jude 1:11-13

This is a grim description of false teachers, yet we encounter them across the landscape. How do we recognize them? By knowing the Bible. Paul warned us:

> *But though we, or an angel from heaven, preach any other gospel unto you than that which we have preached unto you, let him be accursed.*
>
> Galatians 1:8

Don't be surprised if there's false teaching in this world - even in the churches. Don't be surprised if there are traditions that are in error bandying about us. We use these heresies to wrestle through and discern what is true. How? By doing our own homework.

Starting the Journey

We often forget that God is not on trial. We are. He is God. He doesn't answer to us. We answer to Him, and we are the ones who face trials and temptations. How do we therefore get started? How do we enjoy our Bibles? I think that if it's not fun, there's something wrong. I've had a lifetime of adventures, but the most exciting adventures of all are those I've made in the Scripture.

As we seek to begin our study of the Bible, a number of questions come up:

- What is the best approach to Bible study?
- Which is the best Bible translation?

- Which is the best study Bible?
- How do we resolve controversial passages?

Let's start with the first question.

Bible Study Approaches

The *verse by verse* study takes a straight path through a Bible book, reading the book from beginning to end and gathering knowledge about each verse or passage along the way. This is an excellent way to learn what the entire Word of God says, and you'll find that you see something new with each read. It takes time to read through the entire Bible, especially while stopping to understand specific verses and their context.

The *topical* Bible study, as the label implies, focuses on a specific subject. For instance, we might take baptism or pride or the spiritual gifts and research the Scriptures about that specific topic. There is a place for topical Bible study, and it's a good way to get a solid grasp of a particular issue that's of interest to us. We can hunt down all the verses in the Bible that deal with baptism or pride or the spiritual gifts and get the "whole counsel of God" on the matter.

Topical studies are great, but it's important to have a strategic grasp of the whole Bible first. If we only do topical studies, it's easy to leave large holes in our knowledge, and that can leave us vulnerable to deceptive ideas.

The *word* study can take advantage of modern computers, which make it easy to pick a word and find every place it's used in the Bible. We find some words are used repeatedly to convey a specific theme. It's interesting to notice every place the Bible uses the words "horn" or "rock," for instance. It's informative to see which passages refer to God as the "LORD of Hosts" or all the Old Testament prophecies about the "branch."

Some people study the *dispensations* of the Bible, that is, how God dealt with people in different times throughout history. They seek to understand the predicaments each different group of people faced and what God asked of them.

Others choose to read the Bible according to specific *doctrines*. There's a place for studying the doctrines of the Bible and developing them as teaching tools. There is a lot in the Bible about justification by grace through faith, for instance. There is also quite a bit about the deity of Christ, sanctification by the Holy Spirit, God's omniscience and so forth. It's important to know why we believe what we say we believe. It's important to read all the verses on a subject and get a balanced view, because some denominations develop doctrines from just a verse or two while ignoring the rest of the verses that give us a more complete view of the situation.

I am going to pick on certain Pentecostal denominations, for instance, which teach that speaking in tongues is the evidence for being filled with the Holy Spirit. We certainly find many occasions in Acts when people were filled with the Holy Spirit and then began speaking in tongues. In those cases, speaking in tongues was absolutely evidence of being filled with the Holy Spirit. However, some denominations have taken these passages further than the Bible takes them, and they have taught that anybody who is filled with the Holy Spirit will speak in tongues. This is blatantly adding to God's words, because the Bible doesn't teach any such thing. In fact, Paul spends 1 Corinthians 12-14 explaining that the Holy Spirit gives different people different gifts, and there is no one gift given to everybody. What's more, he presents speaking in tongues as one of the lesser gifts and prophecy as one of the more important gifts. Paul reminds his readers, however, that love is more vital than any gift, and without love we are just making noise.

This is why I will hammer over and over again about the importance of knowing the whole Bible. It takes time, but in our doctrinal studies, we need to make sure to have a grasp of all the Bible says on a subject and not make our favorite verses mean more than they do. It's easy to do, and it's also why I encourage people not to believe anything just because I say it - or just because another Bible teacher says it. It's important to study the Bible yourself, because we teachers are fallible.

There are yet other types of Bible study. We might make a *biographic* study and study the life of Paul or Peter or James. We might make an *analytical* study and spend hours trying to figure out what a verse really means. This gets academic, but it can be important to do with confusing passages. I am personally a fan of *synthetic* studies, those that put together the whole thing to gain an understanding God's big picture.

Pieces of the Big Picture

Many people have never really studied the Bible before. We've developed a study called *Learn the Bible in 24 Hours* - 24 one-hour sessions - that gives people an overview of the entire Bible. It includes maps and diagrams and helps people learn to navigate their way around the Scriptures. I would recommend starting there, because it offers an overview of each book along with a strategic overview of the whole Bible. Whatever approach you use, the main goal is to develop a strategic grasp of the entire package. I continually want to emphasize the integrity of the Bible's design.

After getting that good solid overview of the Bible, I support verse-by-verse expositional study. We've done expositional studies on every book of the Bible, some more than once. This is the kind of Bible research that "eats the elephant one bite at a time", so to speak. In my lifetime of Bible study, I've found that expositional studies have lasting results in people's lives.

I enjoy topical studies and word studies too, but the backbone of Bible study should be expositional reading that takes people through the entire counsel of God. It prevents us from having gaps - from missing important elements of God's Word. Some denominations focus on doctrinal training and teach people to name "proof" verses that support their doctrines. That's fine if those doctrines truly represent the whole counsel of God. Too often, however, we find that each denomination has its pet doctrines to the neglect of the whole Word of God. We need to be exposed to the entirety of Scripture.

Jesus emphasized the Scripture. One of the first things He did after the Resurrection was go on a seven-mile Bible study with two of his followers on the road to Emmaus. During those two or so hours, Jesus took them through the books of Moses and the Psalms and the Prophets and showed them all about Himself from the Old Testament. He used the whole counsel of God.

Which Book First?

Once you have a good overview of the Bible, pick an individual book to study. Many people start with Genesis, which is a natural beginning point. It is the book of beginnings. The salvation story starts right there in Genesis. Of course, many people have read through the beginning of Genesis fifteen times without going further. It's okay to start somewhere else, and we all have different favorites.

I think one good book to start with is the Gospel of John. As the great saint Augustine stated, "The Bible is shallow enough for a child not to drown, yet deep enough for an elephant to swim." That's a cute way of saying that the Bible (including the Gospel of John) is straight-forward enough for new believers to work through and learn a great deal. Yet, if you have read through the Bible 100 times, it's still possible to make additional discoveries with each new venture through John's Gospel. That's what we would expect of a book that's supernatural; it's inexhaustible.

You might start with Matthew, which is full of Jesus' discourses. Matthew was a tax collector, and he would have had shorthand skills in that trade. It is possible that Matthew wrote down Jesus' sermons verbatim. Matthew also paid close attention to the many Old Testament passages that Jesus fulfilled. His is the Gospel that focuses on Jesus as the Lion of Judah, the Son of David, the Messiah in fulfillment of the Scriptures.

Acts describes the beginning of the Church, while Daniel lays out Gentile history in advance. Daniel and Revelation are closely tied together, and I actually like to start new believers in Revelation. That shocks some people, but I do that because it's the only book of the Bible that has the audacity to say, "Read me. I'm special."

> *Blessed is he that readeth, and they that hear the words of this prophecy, and keep those things which are written therein: for the time is at hand.*
>
> Revelation 1:3

The blessing comes from several sources. Revelation offers wisdom and warnings to help us avoid error. One of the most interesting blessings, however, is that Revelation touches on every other book of the Bible. In its 404 verses, Revelation includes more than 800 allusions to the Old Testament. Revelation is also the wrap-up book of the Bible. Everything that started in Genesis is wrapped up in Revelation with a big ribbon.

Remember, however, that each of us is unique. The Holy Spirit knows you and your particular needs. He knows what would be best for you to dive into, and He will lead you. I encourage you to pray about it and let the Spirit guide you. It may be He gives you an interest in one book over the others. The important thing is to take a book, any book, and go through it verse by verse. When you are finished with the first book, go on to another one.

Chapter 6
Which Translation

In today's world of computer technology, it's not hard to get serious about the Bible. There are a variety of programs and sites that make it easier than ever to reach into the Hebrew and Greek without knowing Hebrew or Greek. Sites like BlueLetterBible.org and Biblehub.com offer verses in a range of versions, with the original languages and commentaries readily at one's finger tips.

People like to ask me which translation they should read. I tell them I finally found the version I like best, and they lean forward eagerly. Then I hold up my Bible and point out that it's a large print version. Senility is a humbling thing.

The New International Version is popular for many people. It's very readable, and for a new believer it's a great place to start. We facetiously call it the "Nearly Inspired Version." I think the New American Standard Bible is terrific. It gives an excellent treatment of the Greek verbs in the Epistles. I've also used the International Standard Version (ISV). Each of these has its advantages, but I'm sure there will be other new versions in a few years.

I started out with the King James Version. I've gone through virtually all of them, and I've come back to the King James for a variety of reasons. Every translation from the Hebrew or the Greek to English has problems. Certain idioms and nuances just do not translate from one language to another. The translators had to ask themselves how precise they were going to be and how they would treat figures of speech. Those things raise issues. The good news about the King James Version is the issues are well known and well documented. Several modern versions will "translate" by interpreting a text and giving us their interpretation of what it means. The King James is fairly literal in its translation from the Hebrew and Greek, leaving the interpretation up to us.

The English language has changed a little bit since 1611, and it's not as easy to read the King James. The New King James attempts to remedy some of the archaic word use, while still giving a fairly straight forward translation. However, I always do my memory work in the King James. It's a standard, and it has a certain majesty about it.

I was on a Scripture memory kick when the Revised Standard Version came out, and I was well advised to avoid it. It's fallen into some disrepute. There will be problems with any translation, but we know the issues with the King James. King James study Bibles include footnotes that offer alternative meanings or questions of accuracy.

There will be ever new modern translations that will be more modern than the last modern ones. I'm grateful I did my memorization work in a version that will be around fifty years from now.

Textus Receptus

There's another reason I prefer the King James. The KJV translators used the *Textus Receptus* as their primary Greek source. There were 5,556 manuscripts available to the King James translators, and they leaned primarily on the *Textus Receptus*, which had been put together by Erasmus of Rotterdam from Greek texts used by the Byzantine Church. In recent years, it's been popular for translations of the New Testament to be made based on three older texts from the 4th and 5th centuries. These three codices, *Alexandrinus, Vaticanus and Sinaiticus*, are called the "Alexandrian codices." It sounds good to say, "they are older texts." The problem is that the Alexandrian codices survived since the 4th century because they weren't *used*. They are dreadful transcriptions filled with copyist errors, and there are places it appears the scribes doing the copying were exhausted and trying not to fall asleep - or else were terribly sloppy.

A professor of divinity at Oxford, John William Burgon (1813-1888), made a trip to the Vatican to read *Vaticanus* "Codex B" himself. He also studied *Sinaiticus* firsthand, and he was not impressed with them at all. Burgon denounces *Vaticanus*, saying:

> It is undeniable ... that for the last quarter of a century, it has become the fashion to demand for the readings of Codex B something very like absolute deference. The grounds for this superstitious sentiment, (for really I can describe it in no apter way,) I profess myself unable to discover. Codex B comes to us without a history, without recommendation of any kind, except that of its antiquity. It bears traces of careless transcription on every page. The mistakes with the original transcriber made are of perpetual recurrence.[36]

Burgon blames the many missing verses or half verses in the codex on "oscitancy" - on the dullness of a tired copyist who is yawning more than he is paying attention. Burgon continues:

> [I]n the Gospels alone, Codex B leaves out words or whole clauses no less than 1,491 times...accounted for by the proximity of a "like" ending... On the other hand, I can testify to the fact that the codex is disfigured throughout with repetitions. The original scribe is often found to have not only written the same words twice over, but to have failed whenever he did so to take any notice with his pen of what he had done."[37]

We also find that there was a serious problem with Gnosticism in Alexandria in those days. The Gnostics had doctrinal ideas that conflicted with the New Testament writings, and they would delete passages and verses they didn't like. We go over these issues in depth in our study *How We Got Our Bible*. As a bottom line, I do not depend much on textual questions that are raised because the Alexandrian codices left out or changed passages. I'm convinced that verses were more like to be removed from the New Testament Greek texts - whether purposely or through weary error - rather than the popular idea that verses were added later.

Bible Memory

Psalm 119:11 says, "*Thy word have I hid in mine heart, that I might not sin against thee.*" To hide God's Word in your heart implies that you're going to memorize some Scripture.

Which Study Bible?

A young lady in our ministry has said that she picks her study Bibles according to their treatment of behemoth in the notes of Job 40:15 and of leviathan in the notes of Job 41:1. If the notes say, "a large animal identity unknown" she is willing to buy the study Bible. However, if the notes claim that behemoth is an elephant or a hippo, if they say that leviathan is a crocodile or a whale, she puts the study Bible back on the shelf.

Why is that her litmus test?

She doesn't want a study Bible in which the editors' guesses are presented as fact. She's correct, of course, because any fanciful attempt to identify behemoth or leviathan with existing animals is ludicrous. The text doesn't match any creatures alive today. If the editors are willing to suspend judgment about the identities of behemoth and leviathan, she feels she can trust the rest of their footnotes to be simply honest. Calling behemoth a "hippopotamus" or leviathan a "crocodile" is evidence to her that the editors are willing to force their own presuppositions on their textual notes. Since that's not what she wants, she puts those study Bibles back.

I recommend that you go and look through a variety of study Bibles. Find one you enjoy holding and reading - one that is easy on your eyes, one that is comfortable. Feel free to look at the footnotes and how the editors format them. Try using the Bible's cross references and see if the verses add to your understanding. Feel free to see what they say about behemoth and leviathan.

In the end, pick a study Bible and wear it out.

Mark it up. Get one with wide margins, put your notes in it, and then outgrow it and pick another one. That's the challenge.

The ESV Study Bible is widley considered the best

Chapter 7
Three Phases

Phase One: Reading Plan

I suggest a three-phase program for Bible study. The first thing is to have a reading plan that's different from your study plan.

There are several ways to read the Bible through on a regular basis. You might just sit and read from Genesis to Revelation, a few chapters at a time. I enjoy reading portions of the Old Testament, the New Testament, and the Psalms. When I do this, I use three bookmarks, one for each part of the Bible. Then I move the bookmarks a chapter or two each day. That's a simple way to go at it.

I travel with eight Bibles, a dozen commentaries, and concordances in Greek and Hebrew in a device I can carry in my pocket. We used to carry books, then PDAs. We now have phones that can access the entire world. I do my more serious study on a laptop, but I can also carry a Bible on my phone. I can have seven bookmarks in my digital Bible, and I happen to have one in the Torah, one in the Historical Books, one in the Poetical Books, one in the Prophets, one in the Gospels, one in the Epistles, one in the book of Revelation. I try, imperfectly by the way, to read a chapter from each section each day. When I arrive 15 minutes early for a barber shop appointment or I'm held up in the doctor's waiting room, I read one or two of these bookmarks.

In fact, this is a good method for habitually late people to work on in order to be on time wherever they go. Plan to arrive half an hour early, early enough to read a few bookmarks, knowing you will not be wasting the precious moments in your day. At the best, you'll arrive early and have time to read. If you find you keep arriving just on time, at least you're not late anymore. If this is the case, though, change your strategy and plan to get places an *hour* early. You might get in 15-45 minutes of Bible reading.

By reading several bookmarks each day, I can get through the Old Testament once a year and the New Testament twice a year easily. The bookmarks are handy, but many Bibles have ribbons. Find a Bible with a lot of ribbons, if you like. I find the digital Bible handy, neatly held in a cell phone, especially when I travel.

Phase Two: Book Study

The reading plan is the foundation. Next, I encourage you to take on a Bible book study with resources. Go through a chosen book verse-by-verse. First do a background study on your book of interest, whether it's John or Isaiah or Revelation. Read up on its historical background and context, its author and his purpose for writing it. If there are controversies, research them. There are many scholars who question the traditional authorship and dates for the Bible books. This doesn't mean they are correct.

It's important to realize there is a certain bias against supernatural explanations in academia. Therefore, because Daniel accurately prophesies about kingdoms and events that took place long after he died, secular scholars will date the book of Daniel to the 2nd century B.C. They treat the book as if it were written after those events took place. Don't worry about those scholars. Learn about the historical context of Daniel according to the Bible. He was one of the Hebrew children taken captive during Nebuchadnezzar's first siege of Jerusalem in 606 B.C. Twenty years later, Nebuchadnezzar finally destroyed rebellious Jerusalem and the Temple and took a last wave of exiles to Babylon. There they remained until Cyrus the Great gave a decree in 539 B.C. sending them home (as prophesied in Isaiah 44:26-45:6). Understanding the history of the Babylonian captivity is important when reading Daniel.

When you come across scholars who cast doubt on the prophetic power of the Bible or deny its authors, do not fret. There are many sides to each controversy. Generally, if one scholar argues that Daniel didn't write the Book of Daniel, then there are other scholars who have already done the work to answer those arguments.

I take the position that the internal evidence doesn't support a late date for Daniel. It actually supports the authorship of somebody living in the royal court during the Babylonian and Persian empires, just as Daniel claims.

For instance, the Aramaic of Daniel is old and doesn't match the Aramaic of the 2nd century, BC. Kenneth Kitchen offers no precise date for Daniel's Aramaic, but he states it is consistent with Aramaic written between the 7th and 4th centuries.[38] The Persian words used in Daniel are so old they were mistranslated in the Septuagint. Kitchen says of the Persian used in Daniel:

> In the LXX versions, some four Persian words are so poorly 'translated' that their meanings must have been lost long beforehand; this would argue for a date before the second century BC... The Persian words are Old Persian, not Middle; this indicates no independent borrowing of Persian words into Daniel after c. 300 BC [39]

Kitchen is being generous. Old Persian is dated between 600 and 300 B.C., and if the meanings of the Persian words had been completely lost by the time of the Septuagint, that suggests they were written long beforehand.

It's the Greek that really kills the "2nd Century Daniel" view. Daniel has no influence of Greek words, which we'd expect if it were written during the height of the Greek Empire. Alexander the

Great conquered Darius III and took Babylon in 331 B.C. Greece ruled the known world for centuries, yet Daniel contains no Greek loan words except three musical instruments. That's it. There are no Greek idioms. No other Greek terms. We play pianos and violas, but Italy doesn't rule America. If it did, we'd all use far more Italian on a daily basis. If Greek was the trade language when Daniel was written, it would have contained a variety of Greek loan words.

We also find that Daniel correctly named Belshazzar as king when the young ruler's existence had been forgotten by the time Herodotus published his *Histories* in 425 B.C. It was only after J.G. Taylor found the Nabonidus Cylinders in Ur in 1854 that modern scholarship learned Belshazzar was the firstborn son of the often-absent king of Babylon, Nabonidus. All these things point to an early date for Daniel, long before his prophecies came true.

Most importantly, Jesus tells us that Daniel wrote the book that bears his name. Jesus makes several references to him, always with the attitude that Daniel's book was a book of prophecy.[40] If we know that Jesus Christ is God in the flesh, we should have no worries about the authorship of Daniel.

Research the book you are studying. Learn about its historical background, then read through it verse-by-verse. If controversies bother you, wrestle through those questions and find the answers. There's a place for learning to defend the authority and reliability of the Scriptures. However, the most important thing will always be reading God's Word itself. We want to focus on God's voice - not the voice of dry scholastics who may have missed the point. Before anything else, we need to be reading the Word of God and hearing His heart in every passage.

Phase 3: Research Projects

On top of daily reading and book study, you can do special research projects. There might be an occasion to do a topical study or word study. These are *ad hoc* excursions on top of your base plan. Your base plan is reading it through the Bible on some schedule, whatever works for you. It is also to be involved in a serious verse-by-verse study of one of the books of the Bible. That's the base plan. Beyond that, there are subjects you might study beyond your reading plan.

As you pursue your verse-by-verse Bible studies, word studies, topical studies and so forth, you will be benefited by the multitude of resources available. Others have done tremendous amounts of work putting together lexicons and commentaries and dictionaries. They have spent lifetimes researching so that we can quickly access information with the push of a few buttons.

Chapter 8
Resources

We live in a time when Bible study is easier and more convenient than it has ever been in history. We do not have to ask the priest for a scroll, which must be carefully unrolled in the synagogue - where it remains. We can go down to any book store or even St. Vincent de Paul and buy a Bible. We can have several versions piled on our nightstand, right there for us to grab any time we like. That was possible fifty years ago. Now, we can compare verses in several versions using an app on our phones.

We also do not have to hike the hills of Judea to find out where Bethany is in relation to Jerusalem. Many Bible students would love to do just that, but we don't have to. We do not have to pour over verse after verse, counting words. We don't even have to become fluent in Hebrew (although many Bible students would love to do just that). The hard work of other people has given us wonderful tools that make Bible study so much quicker and less tedious than it has ever been in history.

At the end of this book there is an appendix of a variety of commentaries and dictionaries and

Bible study helps that are available. Some of them have been around more than a century and are well known. Some can be expensive. However, in our era of technology, it's not even necessary to buy the books themselves. I personally like having physical volumes on the shelf beside me, readily available to be pulled down and skimmed through and marked up. However, a large number of commentaries and helps have been digitized. Entire libraries are now available on CD-ROM and by download from the Internet.

There are a wide range of Bible study resources available to us. Let's take a look at some of the different types of helps.

Helps

Concordances

Buy a *Strong's Concordance* or its equivalent. A concordance is an alphabetical list of all the words in the Bible, and it lists where every word shows up. It includes lexicons in the Greek and Hebrew, so that researchers don't need to know Greek or Hebrew to discover what the words mean.

Expository Dictionary

A Bible dictionary is a useful tool to learn more about any subject in the Bible. Bible encyclopedias and Bible dictionaries are roughly equivalent. They give a paragraph or two description of most subjects, like Mount Sinai, or the background of a person, like Nathaniel. If we want to know how many women named "Mary" there were, a Bible dictionary would tell you the number and distinguish between them. There are one volume dictionaries, but they tend to be brief. I happen to like a five-volume set, because I can get my arms around almost any topic.

Bible Atlas

The maps we find in the back of some Bibles are fairly basic. A Bible atlas gives detailed visual aids of the Holy Land during different times in its history. One of the things that distinguishes the Bible from, say, the Book of Mormon, is that the locations in the Bible can be determined and verified. The Bible describes real rivers and lakes, mountains and deserts. We can follow the travels of Abraham or the difficult climb that Ruth and Naomi had to make to reach Bethlehem from Moab. It's not quite as eye opening as personally walking the road to Galilee or to Emmaus, but detailed and well-labeled maps do add scope to our understanding.

Commentaries

Commentaries offer explanations or critical notes on Bible texts. Some commentaries go through a Bible chapter verse-by-verse while others offer general comments about the entire passage.

The best commentary is the Bible itself. In Acts 7, Stephen gives us insights into the Old Testament that we don't find spelled out in Acts 7. The writer of Hebrews gives us understanding we might not have had without his explanations.

Outside the Bible, we find all kinds of commentaries. *Exegetical* commentaries dig into the language of a passage, getting into detail about what it means. There are also *devotional* commentaries that focus on the individual and draw our attention to certain meaningful verses that might apply to us personally. *Critical* commentaries take a scholastic look at the text of the Bible, examining questions about the authorship and composition of the book. These are often very scholarly and include a large number of footnotes. The ones that I really enjoy are the *expositional* commentaries. These expound on the greater meaning of a passage. They work to provide the bigger picture.

Each kind of commentary serves an important role, but the most useful commentary for most of us would be an expositional commentary. I would recommend reading through several different expositional commentaries when you are studying a passage. There are a wide number of them available, and each author will offer different insights. One will catch something another commentator missed. Don't depend on just one commentary. When I tackle a book, I typically go get three or so commentaries and read through them together. The commentary that might be my favorite for Genesis may not be my favorite for Revelation. I get the most fruit from those that specialize. The man who has dedicated himself to Zechariah will have many more details and insights to offer on Zechariah than somebody who is doing a general commentary on every book.

Online Resources

Sites like *Blueletterbible.org* and *Biblehub.com* have commentaries and dictionaries and lexicons accessible by the click of a button. They include commentaries on specific chapters and verses, as well as cross-references - other verses in the Bible that apply to the verse you are reading. They offer parallel versions of verses, allowing us to read different translations next to each other. The Hebrew or Greek texts - along with the definitions of each word and the Strong's Concordance numbers. These are easy to pull up so Bible students don't have to know Greek or Hebrew to start looking into the text itself.

I recommend you try out these two sites named above and play around in them, learning how to find the things you need. I'm sure there are other Bible study sites that are also valuable, but I know these two have a large number of readily available resources.

A range of Bible software is available for your computer, offering resources whether or not the Internet is available. The Logos Bible Software, e-Sword, Libronix and BibleWorks all have strengths. Look into them.

I have the BibleWorks Bible study software downloaded onto my computer. I travel with my laptop, and it contains some 4,000 volumes that I can word search. It has an incredible search engine, and it's fast. I give it complex searches, and it pulls up verses that comply. It's tailored for people who have exegetical interest in the Bible, and it's a great program, but it's also a bit of a financial investment.

I have found e-Sword (e-Sword.net) handy because I can look at the Greek and Hebrew easily and quickly pull up any chapter in a few moments. It has a simple word search available - and it's free. The programmers at e-Sword survive on a faith basis, so it's good to give them a donation as an expression of gratitude for providing an excellent little Bible resource. However, it's freely available to rich and poor alike.

If I want to carry a Bible with me, I just take my phone. I can pull out my phone wherever I am and spend a few minutes reading - whether I'm on an airplane or sitting in a waiting room. BibleHub.com and e-Sword both have apps for the phone. Laridian and Olive Tree also offer pocket Bibles. They sell a whole family of resources for download. Olive Tree is apparently very good. I personally haven't used it but I know many people who do and like it.

Many people commute and have a long drive time. It's now possible to listen to the entire Bible on MP3 in the car on the way to work. It's no longer necessary to buy bulky cassette tapes. The whole Bible can be packed away into files on our phones and iPods.

We can watch sermons on YouTube or pop in a DVD and watch a presentation on any book of the Bible. This is good for those of us who are visual and like to be able to hear and see at the same time. DVDs or MP4 downloads offer maps and graphics and other visual aids that we just don't get through audio alone. DVDs and MP4 downloads are good tools to use for home Bible studies, because the teaching is readily available, but it's possible to pause the study at any time and have discussion time with those in the room.

I have a very practical bit of advice about note taking. Many Bible software programs have a way to keep notes on different passages. However, I have had problems with transferring my notes when I've upgraded from one version to the next, or when I've changed software. It's easier to write up my notes in a writing program - like Word or Corel or Word Perfect - and then save it in a folder on my computer. I do this, and I can easily copy my notes on Ezekiel 38 to a special folder on the Magog Invasion or Russia, for instance, if I need to. As you save your notes, think in advance about the system you will use. You might save notes based on the Bible books and chapters you are studying. You might save notes based on topics.

I have also found that it is useful to make an index in Word. I can have a notes document on Ezekiel 38, but I can also create an index within that document to separate the verse-by-verse notes from the topical notes that apply to that chapter. Use whatever system works best for you. I recommend that you give a little thought in advance to your note-taking system in order to make it easy for you to keep things organized. Computer searches these days make things much simpler than they used to be.

Our Personal Tutor

The key through all of this is to be focused on our personal tutor, the Holy Spirit. Approach each Bible study session prayerfully. The Holy Spirit knows the truth, the purpose, and the personal application of each passage we read. There are humans who have poured their lives into giving us information about the Bible, and their knowledge is extremely valuable. However, the Holy Spirit is our ultimate guide. He will point out things we never noticed, and He will make the Word of God come alive in our lives. As Jesus told the disciples:

> *But the Comforter, which is the Holy Ghost, whom the Father will send in my name, he shall teach you all things, and bring all things to your remembrance, whatsoever I have said unto you.*
>
> John 14:26

Not most things. All things.

> *Howbeit when he, the Spirit of truth, is come, he will guide you into all truth: for he shall not speak of himself; but whatsoever he shall hear, that shall he speak: and he will shew you things to come.*
>
> John 16:13

Jesus conditioned his disciples to recognize that He was leaving so that the Holy Spirit could come. The Holy Spirit would be more effective for the situation. Jesus was able to walk through walls after He rose from the dead, appearing in rooms without going through the doors - yet He was still localized. The Holy Spirit is not localized. He is able to dwell in each one of us, so it was necessary for Jesus to leave and to send the Comforter to us:

> *Nevertheless I tell you the truth; It is expedient for you that I go away: for if I go not away, the Comforter will not come unto you; but if I depart, I will send him unto you.*
>
> John 16:7

Each of us has the opportunity to have the Holy Spirit indwell in our lives.

Thy Holy Spirit is not just "frosting" on our lives. He is our vital source of life and safety and wisdom. Paul warns us that we're in a battle. He gives us our military assessment in Ephesians 6:

> *For we wrestle not against flesh and blood, but against principalities, against powers, against the rulers of the darkness of this world, against spiritual wickedness in high places. Wherefore take unto you the whole amour of God, that ye may be able to withstand in the evil day, and having done all, to stand.*
>
> Ephesians 6:12-13

That's what we're up against. This means that there are supernatural enemies who would distract us and derail us from our Bible studies. We have an imperative to put on the whole armor of God. There are seven pieces, and they are all given to us freely by God. We stand in God's strength, not our own strength. They are His armor - His righteousness, His truth, His Word. We are to put on all seven, not just our favorite pieces, and we put them on before the battle. If we read the rest of Ephesians 6, we find we're supposed to be girded with truth. Our head is supposed to be covered with the helmet of salvation, our chest protected with the breastplate of righteousness, and our feet shod with the preparation of the gospel of peace. We need to carry the shield of faith and the sword of the spirit. Our heavy artillery is prayer. I'll leave it to you to do your homework, find out what these things are really about.

The war has already begun, and we're on enemy turf. It's time we got equipped.

Although the war has been won the daily battle must be fought!

1. The Belt of truth
2. Breastplate of Righteousness
3. Sandals w/ the gospel of peace
4. Shield of faith
5. Helmet of Salvation
6. Sword of the Spirit
7. Prayer- fight on your knees

Chapter 9

Ruth

Now that we've said, "This is how you do it," let's do a small practice run and study an actual book of the Bible. We won't go verse-by-verse for want of room, but we can do a quick overview. I want to use as an example one of the smallest books in the Bible - Ruth. It has just four chapters. Let's take a chapter to do a little macro-study here.

Ruth takes place during the period of the judges, before God made Saul king. In the book we meet Boaz, the kinsman redeemer of Ruth and Naomi. It's easy to miss the fact that Boaz was the son of Rahab the harlot, the same woman who hid the spies Joshua sent into Jericho in Joshua 2.

It was not a righteous, spiritually high time in Israel's history. The Israelites had conquered the land under Joshua, yet they periodically fell in and out of serving God faithfully. They would disobey Him for a time, then He would allow some neighboring nation to conquer them. They would cry out to God, and He would send a leader to save them from their enemies. This sordid pattern took place repeatedly. The Book of Judges ends by stating its general theme:

"In those days there was no king in Israel: every man did that which was right in his own eyes."

Judges 21:25

Tradition holds that Ruth was written by Samuel the prophet. The Book of Ruth is the ultimate love story, one between David's great grandfather from the tribe of Judah and his great grandmother from Moab. College literature classes have taught the Book of Ruth because of its high literary quality as an example of an elegant love story.

Ruth also has relevance on a personal and prophetic level. It turns out that Ruth is an Old Testament book representing the Church. It's a surprise to many to hear the Church is found in the Old Testament.

We all know that Jesus Christ was born in Bethlehem, the city of David. We find out in Ruth that Bethlehem was the city of Boaz, the great grandfather of David. This book is an essential prerequisite to the book of Revelation, which is one reason we stir this up here.

Ruth is made up of four simple chapters:

Chapter 1 - Love's Resolve: Ruth cleaves to Naomi, her destitute mother-in-law.

Chapter 2 - Love's Response: Ruth follows Naomi from Moab back to Bethlehem, and she gleans to provide food for both of them.

Chapter 3 - Love's Request: Ruth listens to Naomi and asks Boaz to marry her at the easily misunderstood threshing floor scene.

Chapter 4 - Love's Reward: Boaz redeems the land for Naomi and takes Ruth the Gentile as his bride.

We often discover in the Bible that names have significance. Names not only labeled people, they represented *who* they were. In Ruth, the names are relevant as well. "Naomi" means "pleasant" or "pleasant land." We find that she becomes an idiom for Israel. "Ruth" means "friendship" or "neighbor" and she becomes an idiom for the Gentile Church.

Ruth tells the story of a young Moabite widow who follows her Jewish mother-in-law, Naomi, to the land of Judah. There Ruth provides food for Naomi by going daily into the fields and gleaning behind the reapers. Every day she faithfully goes out, and every day she brings home grain. She attracts the attention of Boaz, the man whose fields she's been gleaning. It turns out that Boaz is a close relative of Naomi's dead husband, and is therefore a close relative to Ruth by marriage. God's hand is clearly all over what happens in the fields of Boaz.

Boaz admires Ruth for her hard work and good manners, and especially for her selfless devotion to Naomi. He encourages her to remain in his fields, and he orders his workers not to harm her. When Naomi learns of the favor Boaz has shown

Ruth, she's pleased because Boaz is a good man. What's more, he's a near kinsman, he has the power to redeem the land her late husband lost. She encourages Ruth to go lie down at Boaz's feet when he's sleeping after a day of threshing grain. When Boaz wakes up and finds her there, she asks him to cover her with his robe. This is not a proposition. It's worse. It's a proposal of marriage - asking him to put his authority over her. Boaz is pleased and promises her he will take care of everything.

Boaz goes through the necessary process of taking responsibility to redeem all that belongs to his late relative, which includes marrying Ruth. At first there's a small obstacle; there's another kinsman who is even nearer, and this places a temporary puddle in the plotline. Happily, that man doesn't want to marry Ruth, so he sets aside his obligation. Boaz takes Ruth as his wife, and there is great rejoicing.

Besides being a love story, the Book of Ruth teaches us all about the Hebrew custom of the *goel*, the kinsman redeemer. When an Israelite lost his land to debt or trouble, it was the responsibility of his closest relative to buy it back, to keep the land in the family. This was the law of redemption that we find in Leviticus 25:23-28. What's more, if a man died without children, his next of kin was supposed to take his widow as his bride to raise up a child for the dead man. This was the law of levirate marriage in Deuteronomy 25:5-10. We find that Boaz fulfills both of these by redeeming the lost land for Naomi and Ruth and by marrying Ruth and giving her a new life.

The story is completed and we learn that Boaz and Ruth are the great grandparents of King David. It's because of this that Bethlehem becomes the house of David and also why Jesus was born in Bethlehem. There is even more to this little romantic story in the Old Testament. Remember, in Jewish hermeneutics, prophesy is not so much prediction as it is a pattern.

We find a variety of patterns here in Ruth.

The 10th Man

There is a pattern of ten in Biblical generations. Judah's sons Pharez and Zarah were illegitimate, the offspring of Judah with his widowed daughter-in-law Tamar. In Deuteronomy 23:2 we learn that a bastard cannot enter the congregation of the LORD until the 10th generation. The descendants of Pharez are Hezron, Ram, Amminadab, Nahshon, Salmon, Boaz, Obed, Jesse, and David. David is the 10th, and his son Solomon built the Temple.

From Adam to Noah, Noah is the 10th man. From Shem to Abraham, Abraham is the 10th man. From Isaac to Boaz, Boaz is the 10th man. Each of these 10th men give us a picture of salvation. Noah was saved when the rest of the world was judged. Abraham is the pivotal Jew, the beginning of the Jewish race. He was called God's friend. God protected Abraham from sacrificing his son Isaac by providing a ram for the sacrifice instead.

Later, on a hill called Calvary, God would sacrifice *His* own Son, Jesus, but for Jesus there would be no sacrificial ram substitute. Boaz also presents a picture; he is the " kinsman redeemer" (*goel*) who buys back the land for Naomi and marries Ruth the gentile bride, representing the Messiah. Repeatedly, these men in the 10th generations give us a picture of the Gospel.

Kinsman Redeemer

We have a kinsman redeemer. In order to save us from our sins - to undo the wreck that Adam started - the Messiah had to be a kinsman. He had to be from the line of Adam, and he had to be able to assume all the obligations of human beings. That's a trick right there. He had to be a descendant of Adam in order to redeem Adam, yet He had to be sinless.

> *And so it is written, the first man Adam was made a living soul; the last Adam was made a quickening spirit... The first man is of the earth, earthy: the second man is the Lord from heaven.*
>
> 1 Corinthians 15:45,47

We find many parallels in Ruth between Boaz and Jesus. Jesus had to be willing to serve as our Redeemer, and Boaz had to be willing to redeem Naomi's inheritance and marry Ruth. There was another kinsman nearer than Boaz who did not wish to marry Ruth, and he gave up his right. Boaz wanted Ruth, and he gladly served as her redeemer.

Naomi serves as a type of Israel. She's exiled from her land, which has allowed Ruth to enter the picture. Ruth would not have made the God of Israel her God and followed Naomi home if Naomi had not been exiled. Ruth learns of Boaz's ways through Naomi, but Naomi meets Boaz through Ruth. In the same way, the Gentiles learned about the true God through the Jews. The Jews have been exiled, and God has opened the doors for the Gentiles to know Him. While the Messiah came from the Jews, and the Gentile Church knows Jesus as the Messiah through the Jews, the Church knows Jesus and Israel currently does not. Yet, there will be a day that all of Israel will be back in the land and will know Him too.

Ruth serves as a type of the Gentile bride. She's a Moabitess, which was a problem under the Law. Moabites and Ammonites were a cursed people according to Deuteronomy 23:3, but grace accomplished what the Law could not. Ruth does not cling to her people. She clings to Naomi and takes the people of Israel and the Israelite God as her own. Ruth does not replace Naomi. She loves Naomi and cares for her, and through Ruth Naomi finds her redeemer.

The interesting parallels continue throughout Ruth. No matter how much Boaz loved Ruth, he waited for her to move. Ruth confronts Boaz, the near kinsman, and seeks his help. As soon as Ruth makes the first move, though,

Boaz takes charge of the situation. He makes all the arrangements.

While the Jews as a whole do not recognize Jesus as the Messiah, the Jewish community still reads the book of Ruth every year on the Feast of Shavuot, i.e., the Feast of Pentecost. We recognize that Pentecost is forever linked to the birth of the Church in Acts 2, because that was the day the Holy Spirit first fell on the believers. It's appropriate that the book about the redeemed Gentile bride should be read every year on the feast that marks the birth of the Church.

Torah Codes in Genesis 38

There's more. We find the rather sordid story of Judah and Tamar in Genesis 38. It's a strange chapter thrown into the middle of the chapters about Joseph, but it's an important tale in the history of Pharez and Zarah, who populated the tribe of Judah. Even though it's a shameful story for Judah, we still find the names of David's genealogy coded there centuries before the king was born. If we do an equidistant letter search for BOAZ in Genesis 38, we find it coded there at an interval of 49 letters. This might be just an interesting coincidence, except that we also find the name RUTH coded there at 49-letter intervals.

The events of Genesis 38 took place centuries before Joshua, Judges, Ruth or 1 Samuel. Moses wrote down the events of Genesis 38 long before Joshua led the people of Israel into the Promised Land. Boaz and Ruth did not exist at that point.

It doesn't stop there, though. We can find the name of OBED in Genesis 38 at 49-letter intervals, as well as the name YISSHAI (Jesse). Finally, to top them all off, at 49-letter intervals again we can find the name DAVID. This is too remarkable to be a coincidence. Together we have the names of Boaz, Ruth, Obed, Jesse, and David, each with an interval of 49-letters - and in chronological order. Despite the questionable nature of Pharez's conception, his descendants' names were coded in the story of his birth before any of them yet existed. This has staggering implications.

Every word, every place name, every jot and tittle in the Bible is precious. As we find these treasures, we realize that David was purposed in God's heart even before his grandfather Obed was born. Not only that, but the Son of David, Jesus the Messiah, was ordained as our Kinsman Redeemer from the very beginning.[41]

This is just one way we can take a book and look at it both expositionally and prophetically. We find surprises hidden in the crevices of the books we read - hidden treasures that reveal God's eternal power and wisdom worked into the very letters of the Scriptures.

At the same time, there are pitfalls we need to avoid - potholes and dangers in the road. God wants to reveal Himself through His Word, but Satan will seek to twist the words of the Bible for his own destructive purposes.

Genesis 38

1 וַיְהִי בָּעֵת הַהִוא וַיֵּרֶד יְהוּדָה מֵאֵת אֶחָיו וַיֵּט עַד־אִישׁ עֲדֻלָּמִי וּשְׁמוֹ חִירָה׃

2 וַיַּרְא־שָׁם יְהוּדָה בַּת־אִישׁ כְּנַעֲנִי וּשְׁמוֹ שׁוּעַ וַיִּקָּחֶהָ וַיָּבֹא אֵלֶיהָ׃

3 וַתַּהַר וַתֵּלֶד בֵּן וַיִּקְרָא אֶת־שְׁמוֹ עֵר׃

4 וַתַּהַר עוֹד וַתֵּלֶד בֵּן וַתִּקְרָא אֶת־שְׁמוֹ אוֹנָן׃

5 וַתֹּסֶף עוֹד וַתֵּלֶד בֵּן וַתִּקְרָא אֶת־שְׁמוֹ שֵׁלָה וְהָיָה בִכְזִיב בְּלִדְתָּהּ אֹתוֹ׃

6 וַיִּקַּח יְהוּדָה אִשָּׁה לְעֵר בְּכוֹרוֹ וּשְׁמָהּ תָּמָר׃

7 וַיְהִי עֵר בְּכוֹר יְהוּדָה רַע בְּעֵינֵי יְהוָה וַיְמִתֵהוּ יְהוָה׃

8 וַיֹּאמֶר יְהוּדָה לְאוֹנָן בֹּא אֶל־אֵשֶׁת אָחִיךָ וְיַבֵּם אֹתָהּ וְהָקֵם זֶרַע לְאָחִיךָ׃

9 וַיֵּדַע אוֹנָן כִּי לֹּא לוֹ יִהְיֶה הַזָּרַע וְהָיָה אִם־בָּא אֶל־אֵשֶׁת אָחִיו וְשִׁחֵת אַרְצָה לְבִלְתִּי נְתָן־זֶרַע לְאָחִיו׃

10 וַיֵּרַע בְּעֵינֵי יְהוָה אֲשֶׁר עָשָׂה וַיָּמֶת גַּם־אֹתוֹ׃

11 וַיֹּאמֶר יְהוּדָה לְתָמָר כַּלָּתוֹ שְׁבִי אַלְמָנָה בֵית־אָבִיךְ עַד־יִגְדַּל שֵׁלָה בְנִי כִּי אָמַר פֶּן־יָמוּת גַּם־הוּא כְּאֶחָיו וַתֵּלֶךְ תָּמָר וַתֵּשֶׁב בֵּית אָבִיהָ׃

12 וַיִּרְבּוּ הַיָּמִים וַתָּמָת בַּת־שׁוּעַ אֵשֶׁת־יְהוּדָה וַיִּנָּחֶם יְהוּדָה וַיַּעַל עַל־גֹּזְזֵי צֹאנוֹ הוּא וְחִירָה רֵעֵהוּ הָעֲדֻלָּמִי תִּמְנָתָה׃

13 וַיֻּגַּד לְתָמָר לֵאמֹר הִנֵּה חָמִיךְ עֹלֶה תִמְנָתָה לָגֹז צֹאנוֹ׃

14 וַתָּסַר בִּגְדֵי אַלְמְנוּתָהּ מֵעָלֶיהָ וַתְּכַס בַּצָּעִיף וַתִּתְעַלָּף וַתֵּשֶׁב בְּפֶתַח עֵינַיִם אֲשֶׁר עַל־דֶּרֶךְ תִּמְנָתָה כִּי רָאֲתָה כִּי־גָדַל שֵׁלָה וְהִוא לֹא־נִתְּנָה לוֹ לְאִשָּׁה׃

15 וַיִּרְאֶהָ יְהוּדָה וַיַּחְשְׁבֶהָ לְזוֹנָה כִּי כִסְּתָה פָּנֶיהָ׃

16 וַיֵּט אֵלֶיהָ אֶל־הַדֶּרֶךְ וַיֹּאמֶר הָבָה־נָּא אָבוֹא אֵלַיִךְ כִּי לֹא יָדַע כִּי כַלָּתוֹ הִוא וַתֹּאמֶר מַה־תִּתֶּן־לִּי כִּי תָבוֹא אֵלָי׃

17 וַיֹּאמֶר אָנֹכִי אֲשַׁלַּח גְּדִי־עִזִּים מִן־הַצֹּאן וַתֹּאמֶר אִם־תִּתֵּן עֵרָבוֹן עַד שָׁלְחֶךָ׃

18 וַיֹּאמֶר מָה הָעֵרָבוֹן אֲשֶׁר אֶתֶּן־לָּךְ וַתֹּאמֶר חֹתָמְךָ וּפְתִילֶךָ וּמַטְּךָ אֲשֶׁר בְּיָדֶךָ וַיִּתֶּן־לָּהּ וַיָּבֹא אֵלֶיהָ וַתַּהַר לוֹ׃

19 וַתָּקָם וַתֵּלֶךְ וַתָּסַר צְעִיפָהּ מֵעָלֶיהָ וַתִּלְבַּשׁ בִּגְדֵי אַלְמְנוּתָהּ׃

20 וַיִּשְׁלַח יְהוּדָה אֶת־גְּדִי הָעִזִּים בְּיַד רֵעֵהוּ הָעֲדֻלָּמִי לָקַחַת הָעֵרָבוֹן מִיַּד הָאִשָּׁה וְלֹא מְצָאָהּ׃

21 וַיִּשְׁאַל אֶת־אַנְשֵׁי מְקֹמָהּ לֵאמֹר אַיֵּה הַקְּדֵשָׁה הִוא בָעֵינַיִם עַל־הַדָּרֶךְ וַיֹּאמְרוּ לֹא־הָיְתָה בָזֶה קְדֵשָׁה׃

22 וַיָּשָׁב אֶל־יְהוּדָה וַיֹּאמֶר לֹא מְצָאתִיהָ וְגַם אַנְשֵׁי הַמָּקוֹם אָמְרוּ לֹא־הָיְתָה בָזֶה קְדֵשָׁה׃

23 וַיֹּאמֶר יְהוּדָה תִּקַּח־לָהּ פֶּן נִהְיֶה לָבוּז הִנֵּה שָׁלַחְתִּי הַגְּדִי הַזֶּה וְאַתָּה לֹא מְצָאתָהּ׃

24 וַיְהִי כְּמִשְׁלֹשׁ חֳדָשִׁים וַיֻּגַּד לִיהוּדָה לֵאמֹר זָנְתָה תָּמָר כַּלָּתֶךָ וְגַם הִנֵּה הָרָה לִזְנוּנִים וַיֹּאמֶר יְהוּדָה הוֹצִיאוּהָ וְתִשָּׂרֵף׃

25 הִוא מוּצֵאת וְהִיא שָׁלְחָה אֶל־חָמִיהָ לֵאמֹר לְאִישׁ אֲשֶׁר־אֵלֶּה לּוֹ אָנֹכִי הָרָה וַתֹּאמֶר הַכֶּר־נָא לְמִי הַחֹתֶמֶת וְהַפְּתִילִים וְהַמַּטֶּה הָאֵלֶּה׃

26 וַיַּכֵּר יְהוּדָה וַיֹּאמֶר צָדְקָה מִמֶּנִּי כִּי־עַל־כֵּן לֹא־נְתַתִּיהָ לְשֵׁלָה בְנִי וְלֹא־יָסַף עוֹד לְדַעְתָּהּ׃

27 וַיְהִי בְּעֵת לִדְתָּהּ וְהִנֵּה תְאוֹמִים בְּבִטְנָהּ׃

28 וַיְהִי בְלִדְתָּהּ וַיִּתֶּן־יָד וַתִּקַּח הַמְיַלֶּדֶת וַתִּקְשֹׁר עַל־יָדוֹ שָׁנִי לֵאמֹר זֶה יָצָא רִאשֹׁנָה׃

29 וַיְהִי כְּמֵשִׁיב יָדוֹ וְהִנֵּה יָצָא אָחִיו וַתֹּאמֶר מַה־פָּרַצְתָּ עָלֶיךָ פָּרֶץ וַיִּקְרָא שְׁמוֹ פָּרֶץ׃

30 וְאַחַר יָצָא אָחִיו אֲשֶׁר עַל־יָדוֹ הַשָּׁנִי וַיִּקְרָא שְׁמוֹ זָרַח׃ ס

בֹּעַז Boaz

רוּת Ruth

עֹבֵד Obed

יִשַׁי Yishay (Jesse)

דָּוִד David

בֹּעַז	Boaz
רוּת	Ruth
עֹבֵד	Obed
יִשַׁי	Jesse
דָּוִד	David

All in 49-letter intervals; & All in chronological order!

Chapter 10
Avoiding Pitfalls

As we do our Scripture study, there are some basic mistakes we can make, and there are at least seven common pitfalls that we want to avoid. These are problems we can get ourselves into by approaching the Bible unwisely. We should always open every Bible study prayerfully. Even now, let's bow our hearts:

Father, thank You for this time of learning. We're grateful that there are no accidents in your kingdom, and all things work together for good for those who are in Christ Jesus and called according to Your purpose. (Romans 8:28) Father, we simply ask that Your excellent and wonderful *will* be accomplished in each of our lives, as we commit ourselves and this time into your hands in the name of Yeshua, our Lord and Savior, Jesus Christ. Amen.

Pitfall 1: Analysis Paralysis

Analysis paralysis is what I call a "head trip." It's going at the Bible with only analytical purposes in sight. We absolutely want our Bible study to be intellectually satisfying, but we can focus so much on accumulating data that we forget to recognize the value. Analysis paralysis is when we gather information but leave our spirits behind. In our intellectual pursuits, we must be careful not to abandon the relevance of the Bible to our spiritual lives and our daily walk with Christ. *Relevance* is the golden chain that binds it together. Studying the Bible is both an intellectual and a spiritual pursuit.

This means we need to ask ourselves some questions as we read the Bible. When we dive into any topic, we can ask, "How does this relate to Christ?" We can ask, "Holy Spirit, what would You show me in this?" The answers to those questions might not pop up right away, but we always keep them in our hearts. We are reading the Bible because we want to know God - we want to know Christ better. We want to understand His heart and His purposes and His way of doing things.

It's astonished me at times to discover that every major problem I've encountered in the Bible yield and unravel themselves when I put Jesus Christ right in the middle. Remember, I'm a businessman. I spent most of my executive career in the business world, in the boardrooms of America. In the business world, it's not what you know that matters as much as *who* you know. The same thing is true of the Bible. When we know Jesus Christ, we can cut through problems that baffle those who don't know Him.

After we ask how our study relates to Christ, we need to ask how it relates to you and me personally. This is the "so what?" question.

How does it impact us? How does it change our priorities and/or our life?

In the case of Ruth, for instance, we see that Boaz is a type of Jesus Christ, our Kinsman Redeemer, and we can glean something about Christ's love and care for us in its pages. We see that Ruth pleased Boaz by her selflessness and care for her mother-in-law, and we should live our lives with the same attitude of selfless love. There are practical implications to the things we read.

When I go through the Bible in my commentaries, I love to take wonderful excursions, if for no other reason than to give those reading/listening a respect for the adventure of it all. The ultimate reason for Bible study, however, is always *how the Word of God impacts our lives.* Learning is defined as "the modification of behavior." If these studies aren't modifying our behavior and leading us in looking more like Jesus Christ, then something critical is lacking. We must always enter every study prayerfully, with a heart to grow closer to God.

Pitfall 2: Textual Doubts

There is a general rule of thumb in research that wisdom is found in many counselors. We can analyze the dickens out of something, but we should always seek out the ideas and thoughts of others who are knowledgeable in the area of our present study. This is especially true in the realm of Bible study, because there will be scholars who approach the Bible from a position of disbelief, and it's important to realize that their skepticism has already been answered by other scholars who approach the Bible from an educated and well-founded position of belief.

As we do biblical research, we encounter studies that will tend to cloud our confidence in the Scripture. Skeptics abound, and they sometimes have PhDs. For instance, the Lutheran theologian Julius Wellhausen popularized the Documentary Hypothesis - the idea that the first five books of the Bible were written down by various scribes and not by Moses. As a young student of the Bible in my teens, I stumbled into this view by Wellhausen and others, which had become wide-spread in the 19th Century and is still taught in many circles today.[42]

The ideas of the Documentary Hypothesis had been developing among 19th century scholars for some time, and Wellhausen built his view from men like Karl Heinrich Graf, Hermann Hupfeld, and Eduard Eugène Reuss. These men suggested that there were four sources for the Torah, all finally brought together by the priests during the time of Ezra in the fifth century B.C. The oldest source was called the Jahwist (Yahwist) source, supposedly written during the time of Solomon and containing the portions of the Torah in which God was called "Yahweh." The Elohist source was allegedly added to the Jahwist source during the time of the Northern Kingdom, and it contained passages in which God was called "Elohim." The Deuteronomist source was found in the book of Deuteronomy, and Wellhausen saw this document as a reflection of the prophets. It was therefore dated to the reign of Josiah in the seventh century B.C., shortly before the Babylonian captivity. Finally, the Priestly source added the ritual and sacrificial portions of the Law, and the priests edited the Torah into its final form under Ezra. The Documentary Hypothesis is also called the JEDP Theory after these sources (J) Jahwist, (E) Elohist, (D) Deuteronomist, and (P) Priestly.

An array of variations has been made on this basic view that the Torah was the product of many men and not Moses alone (or Moses with final notes by Joshua). The problem with the Documentary Hypothesis and related views is that they're completely speculative. No "Jahwist" source separate from the rest of the Torah has ever been found.

Documentary Hypothesis proponents see what they regard as different writing styles or different names for God used, but they're reading into the text what is in their imaginations. It's not true scholarship at all; it's arrogant skepticism. God is called "Elohim" in Genesis 1 and "Yahweh" in Genesis 2, but we also find that God's relationship with humanity is more personal in Genesis 2. We find both "Yahweh" and "Elohim" used interchangeably for God's name in the Flood story starting in Genesis 6. Sometimes both names are used in the same verse - like Genesis 7:16. It's dubious to split up the Bible into little shreds of documents based on the view that one writer wouldn't have used different names for God.

The Bible's writers often had reasons for changing the titles they gave to the LORD. For instance, we find that Isaiah uses different terms for God based on the role God is taking in the passage. Isaiah calls God, "The LORD of Hosts" when speaking of justice and military matters, and he calls God the "Lord Yahweh" (*Adonai YHWH*) when speaking of God's protection and salvation and tenderness toward His people. ("The names of God in Isaiah" is a fun little topical study you might make on your own. It can offer some worthy insights.) Splitting up the Torah based on what God is called misses the point that Bible writers sometimes used specific names of God to highlight different roles He plays in the world and in our lives.

Moses and the Torah

Now, it's likely that Moses did not write about his own death, and Joshua or a scribe close to Moses added the final words to his five books and updated place names. However, the Bible itself claims that Moses wrote all of it - the Law - found in Exodus and Leviticus and repeated in Deuteronomy - and their wanderings in the desert. Moses wrote it, and it was a final book by the days of Joshua.

Exodus 24:4: ***And Moses wrote all the words of the LORD,*** *and rose up early in the morning, and builded an altar under the hill, and twelve pillars, according to the twelve tribes of Israel.*

Numbers 33:2: ***And Moses wrote their goings out*** *according to their journeys by the commandment of the LORD: and these are their journeys according to their goings out.*

Deuteronomy 31:9: ***And Moses wrote this law,*** *and delivered it unto the priests the sons of Levi, which bare the ark of the covenant of the LORD, and unto all the elders of Israel.*

Deuteronomy 31:24-26: *And it came to pass,* ***when Moses had made an end of writing the words of this law in a book, until they were finished,*** *That Moses commanded the Levites, which bare the ark of the covenant of the LORD, saying,* ***Take this book of the law,*** *and put it in the side of the ark of the covenant of the LORD your God, that it may be there for a witness against thee.*

Joshua 8:31-32: *As Moses the servant of the LORD commanded the children of Israel,* ***as it is written in the book of the law of Moses,*** *an altar of whole stones, over which no man hath lift up any iron: and they offered thereon burnt offerings unto the LORD, and sacrificed peace offerings. And he wrote there upon the stones*

a copy of the law of Moses, *which he wrote in the presence of the children of Israel.*

Joshua 23:6: *Be ye therefore very courageous to keep and to do all that is written in* ***the book of the law of Moses,*** *that ye turn not aside therefrom to the right hand or to the left;*

Throughout the Bible, we find constant references to the Law of Moses. There is no confusion about it in the Old and New Testaments. Moses is always credited with the Torah.

1 Kings 2:3: *And keep the charge of the LORD thy God, to walk in his ways, to keep his statutes, and his commandments, and his judgments, and his testimonies,* ***as it is written in the law of Moses,*** *that thou mayest prosper in all that thou doest, and whithersoever thou turnest thyself:*

2 Kings 14:6: *But the children of the murderers he slew not: according unto that* ***which is written in the book of the law of Moses...***

Daniel 9:13a: ***As it is written in the law of Moses,*** *all this evil is come upon us...*

Malachi 4:4: *Remember* ***ye the law of Moses my servant, which I commanded unto him in Horeb*** *for all Israel, with the statutes and judgments.*

We could make a multitude of arguments regarding the unity of the Pentateuch, the evidence that it is much older than Ezra, and that it was written by Moses himself. We can find a variety of Equidistant Letter Sequences that demonstrate God's fingerprints on the text, which we've documented in several other resources on Genesis. However, we can save ourselves a lot of time by just trusting Jesus Christ on the matter. Jesus credited the five books of the Torah to Moses, and that has satisfied me beyond all the scholastic squabbling. Those who do not believe in Jesus Christ have much bigger issues than the authorship of the Torah. Consider the following verses:

- Matthew 8:4, 19:8;
- Mark 7:10, 12:26;
- Luke 16:29-31; 20:37; 24:27, 44;
- John 5:45-46; 7:19-23

Source critics not only question the Mosaic authorship of the Torah. They question the authorship of the prophetic books, especially those with prophecies that come true long after the death of the named authors. We already mentioned the controversy over Daniel in chapter 7. Let's look at Isaiah.

The Book of Isaiah

Critics love to divide Isaiah into at least two authors. They credit the first 39 chapters to Isaiah, the son of Amoz, but they suggest that an unnamed "Deutero Isaiah" wrote chapters

40-66. "Isaiah son of Amoz" is not mentioned by name in the last half of the book. There is a narrative "bridge" in chapters 36-39, which we could call The Adventures of King Hezekiah. From chapters 40-66, there is a change in style that can even be read in English as well as in the Hebrew. Most importantly, Isaiah mentions Cyrus the Great by name in Isaiah 44:28-45:6, which is significant because Cyrus wasn't born until 100 years after Isaiah died. The Temple was still standing in Isaiah's day. Yet, Isaiah speaks of a future time when the Temple is destroyed, when the people of Israel are exiled. In 539 B.C., 150 years after Isaiah' death, Cyrus walked into Babylon and within a year had made a decree sending the Jews home with encouragement to rebuild Jerusalem and the Temple. Those who are skeptical of predictive prophecy assume chapters 40-66 of Isaiah were written by a second "Isaiah" after the Babylonian captivity.

Is this justified? There are plenty of reasons to defend the traditional position that "Isaiah son of Amoz" wrote the entire book.

First, we find many of the same themes alternating back and forth throughout the entire book. We find Isaiah upbraiding the Jews about idol worship in both halves (a non-issue after the return from Babylon).[43] Isaiah shames his people for their false worship and injustice from the beginning to the end of the book.[44] Significantly, Isaiah uses the term "Holy One of Israel" more than all the other Bible writers combined, and he does so 12 times in chapters 1-39 and 14 times in 40-66.

Isaiah warns of Babylon's future destruction in both halves, which is particularly interesting since Babylon was not the enemy in Isaiah's day; Assyria was the big danger.[45] Yet Isaiah warns of Babylon's fall quite a lot in the first half, the half that even skeptics attribute to Isaiah son of Amoz. (We see similar warnings in Jeremiah 50-51 and Revelation 17-18, which suggests God is really serious about the demise of Babylon.) Isaiah describes the suffering and the victory of the Messiah, the King.[46] He offers comfort, restoration and return from exile.[47] God promises judgment and punishment in both halves and He promises healing and blessing in both halves. The messages in the beginning of the book are the messages in the end of the book.

If Deutero-Isaiah was writing after the Babylonian captivity, we'd expect to find Babylonian "loan words" or the influence of Babylonian vocabulary that we find in Ezra and Nehemiah. We don't find those loan words. We find pure Hebrew. The geography of Isaiah is the mountainous land of Israel, not the alluvial plain of the Fertile Crescent.

Even in the English, it's possible to tell that Isaiah was a brilliant writer. We cannot appreciate his skill in Hebrew poetry, but we can recognize his excellent use of imagery and description, his irony and powerful vocabulary. Isaiah is known as one of the greatest writers of the ancient world, and his skill continues throughout the book. What's more the Dead Sea Scrolls do not even have a line break between chapter 39 and 40. In his book *The Unity of Isaiah*, Oswald Allis makes a little dig, "Obviously the scribe was not conscious of the alleged fact that an important change of situation, involving an entire change of authorship, begins with chapter 40."[48]

Skeptics may insist that true predictive prophecy doesn't exist. The actual internal evidence of Isaiah, however, best fits a single, brilliant author who lived in Israel during the time of the divided kingdom before the Babylonian captivity. Why should we be surprised that his prophecies take place? He claims to serve the God who "*confirmeth the word of his servant, and performeth the counsel of his messengers*"[49]

When I get to heaven, I want to give John a big hug. John gave me a verse that was a precious reprieve from boring library research. He quoted from both halves Isaiah in two breaths, attributing them both to the same man. In John 12:38-41, he quotes both from Isaiah 53 and from Isaiah 6. This precious jewel tells me the Holy Spirit doesn't need me to waste my time wandering through dusty libraries, wading through these ill-conceived skeptical arguments, no matter how erudite they sound. John gives us the plain truth. I love that.

The Bible is a complete story. Isaiah didn't prophesy alone. His words coincide with the words of Jeremiah and Ezekiel and Micah. We find the same God speaking through all these great prophets of old, giving the same message in a multitude of ways. The New Testament quotes the Old Testament extensively, and a study of Revelation will take us through the Old Testament, because Revelation has more than 800 Old Testament allusions. The Bible is an integral book. It's one story from beginning to end, and Jesus Christ is the center of it all. That's something that the textual critics can never touch.

Chapter 11
More Pitfalls

Pitfall 3: Relying on Church History

I do not want to knock Church History. It's always good to know the past, but we don't want to draw our conclusions from its errors. We trust the teachings of the apostles who followed Jesus Christ and were filled with the Holy Spirit, but error quickly crept into the early Church. We know this, because Jesus already had to give report cards to seven major churches in Revelation 2-3. Some were doing well, but some were doing very badly.

We all admire St. Augustine, and he was an influential writer in the fifth century after Christ. However, he tended to use the hermeneutics of Origen, who liked to allegorize the Scriptures rather than treat them as true history. Augustine also lived during a time when pastors were being paid by the state. It was not popular to preach from the pulpit that God would return to the earth to rid the world of its evil rulers. He therefore formulated the position that Christ' millennial reign would not be a literal reign from David's throne. Christ would reign in our hearts, and that was the end of it.

Of course, that view implies that God has failed to uphold His promises to the physical descendants of Abraham, Isaac, and Jacob.

Hermeneutics is important. The Old Testament is filled with promises to the children of Israel. It was easy to spiritualize them away during much of the past 2000 years, because the Temple was destroyed and the Jews were scattered across the earth. Then, in 1948 the State of Israel burst back into existence. Jerusalem became the capital of Israel once again. We can see now the possibility of a literal reign of Jesus Christ as the Messiah from Jerusalem. However, God's plan never changed - only our perspective.

We tend to spiritualize the destruction of the city of Babylon. Babylon was never destroyed like it is described in Isaiah 13-14, Jeremiah 50-51, and Revelation 17-18. These chapters describe a sudden destruction that takes place in a day - a great and violent overthrow of the city - whose burning can be seen from the ocean. That's never happened. Babylon just deteriorated into the sands of the desert over the centuries. We tend to allegorize these chapters, and there are some good arguments for suggesting that "Babylon" is in fact Rome, or Mecca, or Paris. However, it may be that "Babylon" is actually Babylon, the pride of the Chaldeans in its old spot on the Euphrates River. That city in all its glory doesn't exist now, but that doesn't prevent its re-emergence as a world power sometime in the future.

The Old Testament repeatedly promises that the Messiah will rule on the earth from the throne of David. Gabriel reaffirmed this to Mary before Jesus was conceived, promising her:

> *He shall be great, and shall be called the Son of the Highest: and the Lord God shall give unto him the throne of his father David:*
>
> Luke 1:32

The throne of David did not exist in Jesus' day, and it doesn't exist today. However, we see that Israel is literally back in the land, fulfilling God's promise in Isaiah 11:11 to gather the children of Israel "a second time." We anticipate that the rest of the chapter will be literally fulfilled as well. There is absolutely a kingdom for the Messiah in the future. Yet, the Church historically has allegorized those passages. Until the past century, the Church has been guilty of terrible anti-Semitism. We don't have to follow the errors of Church history.

God told Abraham in Genesis 12:3, "*And I will bless them that bless thee, and curse him that curseth thee: and in thee shall all families of the earth be blessed.*" The Jewish leaders of the first century rejected Jesus as the Christ, but God still has a plan and purpose for Israel. Yet, because of amillennialism - the view that Christ's millennial reign is figurative and not literal - the Church doesn't realize Israel's role in God's big picture, and anti-Semitism is on the rise again.

Not all early Church fathers taught an allegorical view of Scripture. Irenaeus and some others took a literal view. Throughout history there have been those who spoke against amillennialism, including Sir Isaac Newton, by the way. However, the important point is that the views of the early Church fathers cannot be considered Holy Spirit inspired. They were free to take their positions, but that doesn't mean we are required to agree with them.

Emperor Constantine was officially (whether spiritually or not) converted in A.D. 312, and his Edict of Milan in A.D. 313 legalized Christianity throughout the realm. Constantine's successor Emperor Theodosis subsequently made Christianity the state religion. With the gain of respectability, the Church lost its expectations of an imminent return of Christ. It's okay to study the Bible for ourselves and not blindly follow the early Church fathers.

Pitfall 4: Not Rightly Dividing God's Word

Paul told his protégé Timothy:

> *Study to shew thyself approved unto God, a workman that needeth not to be ashamed, rightly dividing the word of truth.*
>
> 2 Timothy 2:15

What on Earth does he mean? It's important to handle God's Word well - to cut it straight. That requires knowing God's Word inside and out, but it also means approaching Bible study to serve God and grow in knowledge of Him - and *not* to start fights. In the verse prior to this one, Paul urges Timothy to charge others not to strive over words - to no value. The study of the Bible should not be a source for arguments and division. In verse 23, Paul tells Timothy, "*But foolish and unlearned questions avoid, knowing that they do gender strifes.*"

This is similar to his instructions in Titus 3:9, where Paul says: *But avoid foolish questions, and genealogies, and contentions, and strivings about the law; for they are unprofitable and vain.*" It also reminds us of Romans 14:1, where he encourages, "*Him that is weak in the faith receive ye, but not to doubtful disputations.*"

Does this mean we no longer care about what is true? Of course not. When Paul tells Timothy to "*shun vain and profane babblings*" in that same passage in 2 Timothy 2, he is warning him against bad teachings. The "vain and profane babblings" are specifically directed at two particular men who had been wrongly telling people the (final) resurrection had already taken place.

There are certain things in the Bible that are solid - things that God has made quite clear. We stand on certain principle doctrines. Jesus is the Son of God, God in the flesh, through whom the worlds were made. He died on the cross and rose again. He ascended into Heaven where He sits at the right hand of God the Father, and He is coming back. God resists the proud but gives grace to the humble. Idolatry is a no-no. God loves us and is completely trustworthy. The Bible states these things very clearly, and those who oppose these basic teachings are in serious error.

There are other puzzles we're all trying to figure out that can be fruitful studies, but shouldn't cause division. If God is sovereign, do we still have free will? How should we treat the Sabbath day? Whether people should drink wine, or whether women should have long hair - these are not worth fighting over. These types of questions fall into the Romans 14 category. That is, there are questions we can treat with grace. In Romans 14, Paul gives us basic instructions: 1) Do what you believe is right. 2) Don't judge your neighbors in these matters, because they answer to God and not you. 3) Love your neighbors and don't lead them to stumble.

Paul finishes the chapter to Timothy with the heart of the matter:

> *And the servant of the Lord must not strive; but be gentle unto all men, apt to teach, patient, In meekness instructing those that oppose themselves; if God peradventure will give them repentance to the acknowledging of the truth; And that they may recover themselves out*

of the snare of the devil, who are taken captive by him at his will.

2 Timothy 2:24-26

Dispensations

We can look at Paul's words in 2 Timothy another way as well. When Paul tells Timothy to "*rightly divide the Word of Truth*" it brings to my mind the various dispensations - specific time periods in history. We divide history into seven ages, starting with Adam and continuing to the Millennium. First, there was the *Age of Innocence* before the Fall, and then the *Age of Conscience* up until the Flood. This was followed by the *Age of Human Government*, which was developing at that point in history. Abraham began the *Age of Promise*. The *Age of the Law* started with Moses and the giving of the Torah on Mount Sinai, and it ended with John the Baptist and the sacrifice of Christ. At *Pentecost* we began the Church Age, and we all look forward to the Return of Christ to start the *Kingdom Age* in the Millennium. Some people call the Church Age the "Age of Grace," but that's misleading because all these periods involved Grace.

This is a classic way of partitioning biblical history in terms of specific ground rules that God laid down for each of these eras. I suggest a few subtle changes to this list. We can treat the Law as part of the Age of Promise, because they're linked together. We also have The Tribulation, which I believe takes place after the Rapture, after the Church Age but before the Kingdom Age.

Jesus Christ understood the Scriptures thoroughly - not just the letter of the Law and the Psalms and the Prophets, but their intent and purpose. We can trust that He rightly divided the Word of Truth, and in more ways than one. Not only did He know the full meaning of each passage, but there is a key occasion when He read only the first part of a verse and didn't finish it. At the synagogue in Nazareth, Jesus was given the scroll of Isaiah, and He read His own mandate from Isaiah 61:1-2:

> *The Spirit of the Lord is upon me, because he hath anointed me to preach the gospel to the poor; he hath sent me to heal the brokenhearted, to preach deliverance to the captives, and recovering of sight to the blind, to set at liberty them that are bruised, To preach the acceptable year of the Lord.*
>
> Luke 4:18-19

If we go back to Isaiah and read the passage, we realize that Jesus didn't finish Isaiah 61:2. He stopped at a comma. After, "*To proclaim the acceptable year of the LORD,*" the verse continues with, "*and the day of vengeance of our God;*" but Jesus didn't read that part. The day of God's vengeance is the Day of the Lord, which we don't see until Revelation.

It's illuminating to notice what Jesus did not read. He stopped at the comma, and that comma has lasted 2,000 years. The first part was the mandate for the first time He came, and the rest is His mandate for His return. I mention this because this is an example where rightly dividing the Word of Truth is crucial. The Jews didn't realize that the Messiah would come two times - the first to die as the suffering servant of Isaiah 53, and the second time to come as the reigning King of Isaiah 11. They were only anticipating the Messiah's conquest, when He would come to rule on David's throne as the Lion of Judah, and so they missed recognizing Him when He came as the Passover Lamb.

The Jewish rabbis saw two different Messiahs portrayed in the Old Testament. They called one Meshiach ben David and the other Meshiach ben Yosef, the first from the tribe of Judah and the second from the tribe of Ephraim, the son of Joseph. One of these Messiahs would be killed, and the other would become the reigning King. The rabbis didn't realize that these were just two different appearances of the same man.

We are in sort of the same boat here in the Church Age. I believe that Jesus returns two times and not just once. I believe He comes first to gather His Church in advance of the wrath He will pour out on the world, and then I believe He'll return at the end of the Tribulation on behalf of Israel to set up His kingdom. We have a book called *The Rapture* which goes over these things in more detail. Of course, there are other Bible teachers who believe that Jesus only comes once at the end of the Tribulation. There are a variety of views, and this is the type of topical study you might undertake on your own. You can research the differing views on the matter and come to your own conclusions based on your honest reading of the text.

Resolving Power

Let's consider another set of passages. Most people assume that Matthew 24 and Mark 13 and Luke 21 are the same presentation. They do include some overlaps, and Matthew and Mark's versions are virtually the same with one verse difference. Matthew 24 and Luke 21 are also very similar, but they are two different presentations to different people at different times and so we see in them some subtle distinctions. It's like looking through a good telescope at a bright star only to realize with the greater resolving power that you were actually seeing a binary star system.

Both Matthew 24 and Luke 21 include a group of events that Matthew labels "the beginning of sorrows" or the beginning of birth pangs. Both of them talk about wars, famines, earthquakes in diverse places and so forth. Luke describes the things that take place before these events and Matthew covers the things that take place after them. Read these chapters carefully. Luke describes the desolation of Jerusalem that occurred in A.D. 70, while Matthew talks about the desolation of Jerusalem that's yet future. They're different. Yet, both Matthew and Luke ultimately have in view the end of all things - the cosmic upheaval with signs in the sun, moon and stars.

Notice something. Matthew warns about the abomination of desolation in verse 24:15, that when it stands in the Holy Place, those in Judea need to run to the hills without even stopping to grab clothes. He warns that this will lead into the Great Tribulation, which Jeremiah 30:7 calls the "time of Jacob's trouble."

Luke mentions the same wars, famines and earthquakes, but before these things He outlines that the disciples will be persecuted and Jerusalem will be surrounded by armies - which applies to the fall of Jerusalem in A.D. 70. There are people who are confused by these two chapters. They try to synchronize them and fit them into one end-times scenario, or one A.D. 70 scenario, not realizing that the two passages focus on two different series of events.

Chapter 12
The Final Pitfalls

Pitfall 5: Confusing Israel and the Church

This leads to our fifth pitfall. Many people reading the Bible do not realize that the Lord deals with Israel and the Church as separate beings. Each has a unique and separate origin, mission and destiny. Israel is mentioned 75 times in 73 New Testament verses, and I bring this up to smash up the false idea that the Church has inherited the blessings and promises given to Israel. The two are distinctive and mutually exclusive, and lack of understanding has led to such horrors as the Holocaust. Certainly, there were Christian believers like Corrie and Betsie Ten Boom who hid and protected Jews - to their own risk. However, multitudes from allegedly Christian churches turned a blind eye to the genocide of God's chosen people during World War II, because they actually believed the Jews were evil Christ killers and deserved to die.

Jesus says something very interesting in Luke 21:24

And they shall fall by the edge of the sword, and shall be led away captive into

> *all nations: and Jerusalem shall be trodden down of the Gentiles, until the times of the Gentiles be fulfilled.*

There is a "time of the Gentiles" that needs to be completed. Paul makes reference to it in Romans 11:25: "*that blindness in part is happened to Israel, until the fulness of the Gentiles be come in.*"

In Daniel 9, the angel Gabriel gives a prophecy of a period of 70 weeks (of years) that mark the final years until everlasting righteousness and the end of prophecy and the anointing of the Holy of Holies:

> *Seventy weeks are determined upon thy people and upon thy holy city, to finish the transgression, and to make an end of sins, and to make reconciliation for iniquity, and to bring in everlasting righteousness, and to seal up the vision and prophecy, and to anoint the most Holy.*

However, we find out in the next verses that those 70 weeks are not continuous. There are 69 weeks until the Messiah comes - and is subsequently cut off. Then "*the people of the prince that shall come*" will destroy Jerusalem and the Temple, and desolations will follow. There is an interval between the 69th and 70th weeks of Daniel 9 - and Gabriel doesn't say how long it will last. This interval is the Church Age. The Church was born on Pentecost, ten days after Christ's

Ascension. We are still in the Church Age, and it's my belief that when Christ comes to rapture His Church, the "time of the Gentiles" will end, and soon afterward the 70th Week of Daniel will begin.

Those 70 weeks don't apply to the Church. They apply to "*thy people and upon thy holy city.*" Daniel's people were the Jews, the people of Israel. Their holy city is Jerusalem.

There were prerequisites for the birth of the Church: Christ's Atonement on the cross, His Resurrection, and His Ascension. The spiritual gifts were only given after Christ ascended, after He sent the Holy Spirit. The Church is separate from Israel. Israel is the mother of the man-child in Revelation 12:1. The Church is the bride of Christ, as Paul discloses in Ephesians 5:22ff. The Church will be raptured. There are certainly Jews that are part of the Church, just as Paul and Peter and John were part of the Church. But Israel as a group will be saved after the time of the Gentiles.

> *For I would not, brethren, that ye should be ignorant of this mystery, lest ye should be wise in your own conceits; that blindness in part is happened to Israel, until the fulness of the Gentiles be come in. And so all Israel shall be saved: as it is written, There shall come out of Sion the Deliverer, and shall turn away ungodliness from Jacob:*
>
> Romans 11:25-26

These are issues that have to do with eschatology as much as with ecclesiology. It's important to understand the different purposes of and promises to the Church and to Israel.

Pitfall 6: Presuppositions

This next pitfall applies to every area of our lives and not just Bible study. We all save ourselves heartache in our jobs and schooling and relationships if we avoid depending on our own presuppositions. We need to constantly keep our hearts and minds open to the truth, whatever it may be. We don't even recognize our prejudices much of the time. These are the foundational beliefs and positions we take for granted without having ever taken the time to see if they are true. Yet, we go around believing incorrect things all the time, just because somebody misinformed us at one point or another in our lives.

Did you know that daddy longlegs are not poisonous, and daddy longleg spiders (a different creature altogether) aren't known to be toxic to humans, whether their mouths are too small to bite or not? Did you know that the leaves change colors every autumn due to less light, not necessarily due to the cold? Or that reading in low light can make your eyes tired and maybe give you a headache, but won't make you go blind?

People approach the Bible with a variety of incorrect ideas without even realizing it. There is no verse in the Bible that tells us,

"God helps those who help themselves." Proverbs contains plenty of verses against laziness, but we can thank Algernon Sidney and Benjamin Franklin's *Poor Richard's Almanac* (1757) for that little saying - not the Bible.

As we approach the Bible, we need to be careful to set aside our potentially incorrect presuppositions. The first step, however, is simply to recognize that every one of us brings prejudices and preconceptions to the table. Any time we leave the actual text of the Bible and embrace instead our traditions, we get into trouble. The Jews did. Mosaic Judaism came from God, but after the Jews came home from Babylon After Ezra, they began to add their own oral laws and traditions to the written Law of Moses. About the 5th century A.D. those oral traditions were written down as the Talmud. We find in the New Testament that Jesus didn't have a lot of good to say about the traditions the Pharisees, especially when they directly contradicted the Law.

> *But he answered and said unto them, Why do ye also transgress the commandment of God by your tradition? For God commanded, saying, Honour thy father and mother: and, He that curseth father or mother, let him die the death. But ye say, Whosoever shall say to his father or his mother, It is a gift, by whatsoever thou mightest be profited by me; And honour*

> *not his father or his mother, he shall be free. Thus have ye made the commandment of God of none effect by your tradition.*
>
> Matthew 15:3-6

The Pharisees were the professional law keepers of the day. They were zealous and serious about following the Law, yet their minds were so heavily laden with their preconceptions that they couldn't see past the letter of the Law to its heart and purpose. Jesus constantly upbraids them for it. He told the people:

> *For I say unto you, That except your righteousness shall exceed the righteousness of the scribes and Pharisees, ye shall in no case enter into the kingdom of heaven.*
>
> Matthew 5:20

That must have been a blow to the Jews, because if the Pharisees couldn't please God by their diligent law keeping, then there wasn't hope for anybody. Yet, the Pharisees were not dedicated to the heart of God as much as they were to their own ideas, their traditions, their rules and regulations. Talmudic Judaism was followed in the 12th century by the Kabbalists and their mystical interpretations of the Torah. Some Jews venerate the Zohar, a mystical commentary on the Torah, with as much honor as they do the Psalms. Yet, it is a symbolic interpretation of the Torah that seeks to initiate change within God. The Kabbalistic teachings of Abraham Abulafia (1240-1291) seek to initiate change inside the person, but not through contemplation of the plain text of the Torah. Instead, the mystic focuses on the letters of the Torah, rearranging them and finding hidden meaning in them. In the 18th century came Hasidic Judaism with its roots in Kabbalah. Each of these kinds of traditional forms of teaching lengthen the tether between man's traditions and the actual straight forward teachings of the Bible. The Jews began to venerate the rabbis' interpretations higher than the text itself.

The Jews do have a very serious problem. They've lost the Temple. They know that forgiveness of sins requires the shedding of blood, but they cannot perform blood sacrifices because there is no Temple. Since they can no longer depend on the sacrificial system of the Law, they have turned to false, non-biblical views. They need to depend on the whole counsel of God, but they've folded themselves into these bizarre ideas promoted by ancient rabbis.

Pitfall 7: Lacking the Whole Counsel of God

We can take a lesson from those who fall into error. To avoid all these pitfalls, we need to read the Bible as a whole document, one story written by one Author. We need to get a strategic grasp of the entire book. As we approach the Bible prayerfully, seeking the direction of the Holy Spirit, we are working to familiarize ourselves with the whole counsel of God.

Too many churches have their pet doctrines, their favorite teachings to the exclusion of the rest of the Bible. This is dangerous. Neglecting the whole Bible is like a church body that focuses on only fellowship and neglects to do the dishes. Everybody enjoys eating together, but nobody wants to clean up the kitchen.

Imagine eating a diet of only carrots. Carrots are a fine food, but they do not contain all the nutrients a body needs - and if that's all we eat they'll turn our skin orange. What's more, some churches have pet doctrines that aren't that healthy, as though their entire doctrinal focus is eating potato chips and candy corn.

We need to read the entire word of God, else we can turn into people like the Pharisees, who were so dedicated to strict obedience to the law that they tithed even their herbs of anise and cumin, but they failed in the areas of mercy and justice - which were more important![50] We can also err the other way - in which we are so "compassionate" that we allow sin to infect the Church without (prayerfully) addressing the problem. We can get caught up in questions about whether we choose God or whether God chooses us, and neglect to just go out and tell people the good news that Jesus died for us. We can focus so much on evangelism that we fail to feed and care for the believers already in our midst.

We need to suspend judgement about our favorite traditions or human explanations about how to "do religion" and we need to read the Bible for itself. We need to judge every idea according to the whole counsel of God - the full witness of the Bible and not just pieces pulled here and there out of context.

Jots and Tittles

The Bible is the living Word of God. I have discovered that I constantly find something new in its pages, no matter how many times I've read through it. God always has something new for us as we place ourselves before Him every day - and we need to be reminded of things we've already learned (sometimes 10 times) but have forgotten. There are always treasures to be found in each new trip through the Scriptures.

Chapter 13
The Golden Plover

I happen to love a little bird called the golden plover. It starts in Alaska and flies to Hawaii every winter without stopping. It can't swim, and there are no islands for it to stop and rest. It begins the trip weighing about 200 grams, 70 g of which will be burned up as fuel during the incredible 88-hour flight. To make the journey, though, the little bird actually requires 82.2 grams of fuel. Why doesn't it plummet into the ocean after 81% of the distance? Because it flies in formation - each bird taking turns being the lead bird with all the head wind. This saves the birds 23% of the energy they need. Yet, they have to make the flight with exact precision. If their heading gets off by even a tiny bit, they'll end up floundering in the Pacific Ocean.

How do they know their way? They have no compasses, no keen instruments to direct them, yet their navigational skills are amazing. I came across this from the writings of Werner Gitt, and it blew me away. As I went down to where Nan, my wife, was making breakfast, I showed her Gitt's information about the golden plover. I said to her, "Have you seen this?

She took one look at it and said, "Gee. That's just like us, isn't it? We can't make it alone either." She cut right through to the "so-what?" question.

We were never meant to go it alone in this world. We need each other.

Small Groups

We should all study the Bible on our own and have our quiet one-on-one time with God, but one of the greatest blessings to growth is small group Bible study. We encourage all of our people to participate in a small group that meets during the week. People who have sat in church for years finally find the Bible come to life when they join other Christians who are hungry to know God and His Word better. In my 60 years of Bible study, I've found the most growth in small groups.

Of course, after joining a Bible study and maturing in the Word for some time, it is beneficial to lead a Bible study. We all learn the most about a topic when we have to teach it. You can do your own research or get a booklet. I'd encourage you to get a commentary DVD and pop it in, then stop it every so often to discuss it with others. We have Bible commentaries on each book of the Bible, but we also have overview studies like Learn the Bible in 24 Hours on DVD. We have topical studies like *Prophecy 101, The Rapture, Daniel's 70 Weeks*, or *Angels* that people would find interesting.

We offer a wide variety of Bible study tools through the Koinonia Institute, including workbooks and leader's guides. Everybody in the group has the opportunity to explore the possibility of university credit with the school of their choice through a KI program. I'll talk more about KI in a moment.

Even if you are not comfortable teaching the Bible to others, however, you might open your home and host a Bible study in which somebody else leads. There are those who have the gift to teach, and there are those with the gift of hospitality. Some people make the Bible come alive to others with their interest and passion. Others make great coffee or brownies or calzones. If you get a set of Bible teachings for people to watch and talk about, and you provide the coffee and cookies, that's a great evening.

There are those who might not want to lead a Bible study, but they can be teaching assistants, helping others go through a study program. We need disciples, but we also need people who make disciples.

People can put together Bible studies on their own, or a church body can choose a facilitator who helps members to start home studies and then encourages and provides assistance to those Bible study leaders. Our online students have a teacher's assistant, but there are a number of different roles involved: small group administrators who serve a small group, meeting coordinators, promoters, media and broadcast folks. As our students grow, they move on into broader areas of service.

There is an interesting and practical model of small home groups that has worked well for large churches where things can get impersonal very quickly. Even though everybody belongs to a large church, they meet in small groups every week. These are people who meet regularly and allow themselves to become vulnerable to each other. They need to be able to trust one another and be accountable to each other. If new members are going to be invited, the group prays about it and all members must agree to add the new members. This does not stymie growth. It keeps the group a blessing to all its members.

One simple rule for this model is that the small group can never grow beyond 12 members. Once the group gets too big, it gets impersonal and no longer feels safe emotionally. If it is going to grow larger, then the group splits up - and each of the 12 members start a second group. They still meet together to study and pray together, but now they each have a second weekly group that they lead. The 12 now have the opportunity to become 144. They still have close, personal study time. They still remain accountable to their original 12, but now they are growing their own group. Once their second group gets to 12 and bursting, its members form 11 new groups.

This continues on and on. The key is that new members cannot be stolen from other groups or other churches. As the group grows, its members are being discipled. Small group study facilitates outreach and study for new believers while still feeding the leaders. This model has the potential to reach entire neighborhoods and towns for Christ - all through the gentle, personal, comfortable venue of a home Bible study.

Home meetings are what we call *The Once and Future Church*. This was the model of the Church in Acts, and it's still the model of the Church wherever persecution takes place. Today under a government that pushes atheistic Communism, house churches are flourishing in China.[51] There are government approved churches in China, but that's not where the fire is. Church fronts existed under the soviets in Russia too, but they did not preach the Gospel.

Even now in America we have church buildings where the people inside won't "*endure sound doctrine*" as Paul warned in 2 Timothy 4:3. J. Vernon McGee predicted that a day would come when the body of Christ would have to go underground, and he meant those of us in "free" countries. He even predicted that those leading the attack against believers would be the denominational churches, interesting enough. Home Bible studies are places where we can dig through the whole counsel of God to build solid doctrine, receive correction and instruction in righteousness, but also encouragement and help in time of need. These meetings should be places of refuge in a world that prefers to go its own way rather than learning God's way.

I've had home groups that were the highlight of my week. I'd have a bit more joy in my spirit on Tuesdays, because it was home Bible study night. We joined together with dear friends to share our hearts, to pray for each other, and to get excited about the Bible together. I look back at those evenings as some of the most precious times of my life.

Chapter 14
Koinonia Institute

We created Koinonia House because we wanted to help people study the Bible. That was the whole reason our ministry was started: "to create, develop, and distribute materials to stimulate, encourage, and facilitate serious study of the Bible as the inerrant Word of God."

We now have two arms to accomplish that mission statement: Koinonia House and Koinonia Institute.

Koinonia House is still one of the largest publishers of electronic materials in the Christian field. We offer a large number of Bible studies and topical teachings, audio and video and text, for free on our website: khouse.org. We also have printed books and e-books, including materials from other ministries in keeping with our core purpose:

We developed a second arm, Koinonia Institute, as a resource for individuals and for small groups. We have an online store where our products can be ordered or downloaded. Many of our products are available as electronic files on the Internet. We also have podcasts of our weekly studies that can be downloaded onto iPods or phones. Members can get to know one another and form online groups that have become sources of friendship along with deeper study and understanding of God's Word. The Institute trains members on three different tracks: the Berean track, the Issachar track, and the Koinonos track.

The purpose of the Berean Track is to turn believers into Bereans, based on Acts 17:11, with the motto: "To receive the Word but search every day to prove what things are true." This is the diligent Bible study track. We generally require Berean Track students to first go through *The Bible in 24 Hours* as an overview. They then go through our audio commentaries book by book, with the potential of studying through the entire Bible.

The Issachar Track is based on 1 Chronicles 12:32:

> *And of the children of Issachar, which were men that had understanding of the times, to know what Israel ought to do; the heads of them were two hundred; and all their brethren were at their commandment.*

The purpose of the Issachar Track is to train people to be like the children of Issachar, who understood the times and knew what their nation had to do. This is the international political arena and prophecy track, if you will. Students on the Issachar Track begin with our study Prophecy 101 and then go through our Strategic Trends. These continue on to become some of our research associates.

The Koinonos track is based in the Third Commandment, found in Exodus 20:7:

> *Thou shalt not take the name of the LORD thy God in vain; for the LORD will not hold him guiltless that taketh his name in vain.*

In Proverbs 30:8-9, Solomon prays that he be neither rich nor poor. If he's too full, he fears he will deny God. He fears poverty as well: "*lest I be poor, and steal, and take the name of my God in vain.*" He didn't want to sin, because he didn't want to take God's name in vain.

I do not believe the Third Commandment is about swearing. I believe it is about representing God well. We are representatives of Jesus Christ. Our behavior reflects on Him. Therefore, the Koinonos track is about serving God well and being good ambassadors for Him.

The Koinonos Track starts off with principles of discipleship and spiritual hygiene. The next step is small group participation and ultimately teaching assistantships. On this track, we tend to lean heavily on my wife Nan's materials: *The Way of Agape, Be Ye Transformed, Faith in the Night Seasons* and others.

These are the three main tracks of the Koinonia Institute.

Two Lakes

There are two lakes fed by the same source. One is surrounded by fruit-bearing trees and a green landscape. The other lake is fed by the same source, but its water is unpalatable and it's surrounded by an unproductive desert. One has become a symbol of life while the other has become a symbol of death. These are real lakes. Both are fed by the same source, but one is full of life and the other is completely dead.

One of these lakes is the Sea of Galilee, which is fed by the Jordan River starting up at snowy Mount Hermon. The other is the Dead Sea, down south at the end of the Jordan River. What is the difference between them? One receives the water that flows down from Mount Hermon, but it passes on what it receives. It passes on the water that is the source of life. That's the Sea of Galilee. The Dead Sea, on the other hand, receives and receives and receives and receives. The water never flows out. It just evaporates, leaving behind the salt that has killed the sea and left the land around it a barren desert.

There are some Christians who attend churches and Bible conferences, and their bookshelves are full of books. However, they never pass on the knowledge they've gained. They don't teach children or teenagers or other adults. They don't share the life-giving water of God's Word.

Which kind of Christian are you? Which kind of Christian are you going to be?

Edward Kimball

I want to finish this book with the marvelous story of Edward Kimball. Edward Kimball is not likely a name you've heard, because Edward Kimball is not famous. He did teach Sunday school, however, and one day he had a burden for one particular young man among his Sunday school students. He obeyed the leading of the Holy Spirit, and he went down to the shoe store where this young man worked. There in the shoe store, Edward led the kid to Christ. That young man was Dwight L. Moody, who later became a great evangelist whose ministry rocked two continents.

While preaching in the British Isles, Moody spoke at a small chapel that was pastored by Frederick Brotherton Meyer. In his sermon, Moody told a very emotionally charged story of his Sunday school teacher whom he knew personally and who went to every student in his class and led them to Christ. The message so impressed Meyer that it changed his whole ministry. He was inspired by that story to become an evangelist. Over the years, Meyer came to America several times to preach. Once in Northfield, Massachusetts, a confused young preacher sitting in the back row heard Meyer say the following, "If you're not willing to give everything to God, are you willing to be *made* willing?" That remark inspired young J. Wilbur Chapman, who became one of the most effective evangelists of his time.

There was a volunteer who helped Chapman set up chairs in his crusades. This volunteer learned to preach by watching Chapman over the many sessions of the crusades where he volunteered.

This young man eventually took over Chapman's ministry, and he became one of the most effective evangelists of the 20th century. His name was Billy Sunday. In the great arenas of America, Billy Sunday turned thousands to Jesus Christ.

Inspired by a 1924 Billy Sunday crusade in Charlotte, North Carolina, a committee of Christians committed themselves to reach that city for Christ. In 1932, they invited the evangelist Mordecai Ham to hold a series of meetings. In the huge crowd of one of these meetings sat a lanky 16-year-old kid, spellbound by the message of this white haired old preacher who seemed to be shouting and waving his bony finger directly at him. Night after night, this young guy attended and finally went forward to give his life to Christ. His name was Billy Graham. Billy Graham has probably communicated the Gospel of Christ to more people than any other single human being in the entire world.

All this started because a nobody named Edward Kimball listened to the Holy Spirit and had concern for one of his students. He did what God asked of him and led this young man to Christ in a shoe store. Because of that small act of obedience, Ed Kimball changed the world.

We do not appreciate the value and potential of each person around us. The annoying neighbor whose dog poops in our yard, or the little boy who runs through our flower beds, might have an eternal destiny that would blow our minds.

We don't know the effect that one simple act of obedience to the Holy Spirit can have. We don't realize the ways God wants to use us to change the world. It is possible that somebody you tell about Christ will light a chain reaction that could exceed the one that Edward Kimball started in that shoe store. Without Christ, we can do nothing, but with Him we, can do anything. That's how God has chosen to work.

At Koinonia Institute, we're anxious to help you any way we can. We have individual studies. We can help you organize groups and support you as you progress in a program that will meet the specific area of ministry to which you believe God has called you. We're anxious to help you, because we know you are the hands and feet of God out in the world.

Appendix

Bible Study Resources

Study Bible

Pick out one you like. Make sure the print size is comfortable for you to read. Wear it out and then try another!

Concordances

- Strong, J. (1890). *The Exhaustive Concordance of the Bible*. New York: Abingdon-Cokesbury Press. (Commonly called "Strong's Concordance." Strong numbered and defined each Hebrew word in the Old Testament, and commentaries often use his numbers to reference Hebrew words.)
- Young, R. (1964). *Analytical Concordance of the Bible*. Grand Rapids, MI: William B. Eerdmans Publishing Co.

Handbooks:

- Halley, H.H. (1944). *The Pocket Bible Handbook*. Chicago: Henry H. Halley. (Commonly called "Halley's Bible Handbook.")

Dictionaries

- *The Interpreter's Dictionary of the Bible* (5 vols). Nashville, TN: Abingdon Press, Nashville.
- *The Illustrated Bible Dictionary* (3 vols). Leicester, England: InterVarsity Press.

Encyclopedias

- *The Zondervan Pictorial Encyclopedia of the Bible.* Grand Rapids, MI: Zondervan.
- *The International Standard Bible Encyclopedia* (5 vols). Grand Rapids, MI: William B. Eerdmans Publishing Co.

Bible Atlas

Pick one you like.

Complete Commentary Sets

- Jamieson, R., Fausset, A.R., Brown, D. (1871,1948) *Commentary Critical and Explanatory on the Whole Bible* (6 vols). Grand Rapids, MI: William B. Eerdmans Publishing Co. (My first and still a favorite, it's commonly called "Jamieson-Fausset-Brown's Commentary.")
- Spence, H.D.M. & Exell, Joseph S. (1950). *The Pulpit Commentary* (21 vols). Grand Rapids, MI: William B. Eerdmans Publishing Co.

- Barnes, A. *et al.* (1851, 1983) *Barnes Notes on the Old and New Testaments* (14 vols). Grand Rapids, MI: Baker Book House.
- Keil, C.F., and Delitzsch, F. (1978). *Commentary on the Old Testament* (trans. from the German, 10 vols). Grand Rapids, MI: William B. Eerdmans Publishing Co.
- Meyer, H.A.W., *et al.* (1873-1893) *Critical and Exegetical Commentary on the New Testament* (21 vols). London: T & T Clark. (Better known as "Meyer's Commentary.")

Individual Commentaries (by Book):

My Personal Favorites:

- Barnhouse, Donald G.
- Bullinger, E.W.
- DeHaan, M.R.
- Feinberg, Charles L.
- Ironside, H.A.
- McGee, J. Vernon
- Morris, Henry
- Newell, Philip R.
- Walvoord, John F.
- Wiersbe, Warren

Use all with caution. Remember Acts 17:11!

(Bibliographies are included in the handbooks (study notes) in our Verse-by-Verse Commentary sets.)

Word Studies and Language Helps

- Green, J. (1979). *The Interlinear Hebrew/ Greek English Bible* (4 vols). Lafayette, IN: Associated Publishers and Authors.
- Wigram, G.V. (1979). *The Englishman's Greek Concordance of the New Testament* (Numerically coded to Strong's Exhaustive Concordance). Grand Rapids, MI: Baker Book House.
- Wigram, G.V. (1980). *The Englishman's Hebrew and Chaldee Concordance of the Old Testament* (Numerically coded to Strong's Exhaustive Concordance). Grand Rapids, MI: Baker Book House.
- Brown, F., Drivers, S. & Briggs, C. (1906, 1981) *The Brown-Driver-Briggs Hebrew and English Lexicon* (Numerically coded to Strong's Exhaustive Concordance). Lafayette, IN: Associated Publishers and Authors.
- Brenton, L.C. (1970). *The Septuagint with Apocrypha: Greek and English.* Grand Rapids, MI: Zondervan.
- Gesenius, H.W.F., Tregelles, S.P., tr. (1979). *Gesenius' Hebrew and Chaldee Lexicon to the Old Testament Scriptures* (Numerically Coded to Strong's Exhaustive Concordance). Grand Rapids, MI: Baker Book House.
- Wilson, W. (1978). *Old Testament Word Studies.* Grand Rapids, MI: Kregel Publications.

- Vine, W.E. (1940). *An Expository Dictionary of New Testament Words* (4 vols). Old Tappan, NJ: Fleming H. Revell Co.

Theology

- Shafer, L.S. (1947). *Systematic Theology* (8 vols). Dallas, TX: Dallas Seminary Press.
- Fruchtenbaum, A.G. (1994). *Israelology: The Missing Link in Systematic Theology*. Tustin, CA: Ariel Ministries Press.
- Botterweck, G.J., & Ringgren, H. (1980). *Theological Dictionary of the Old Testament* (4 vols), Grand Rapids, MI: William B. Eerdmans Publishing Co.
- Kittel, G., & Friedrich, G. (1976). *Theological Dictionary of the New Testament* (10 vols). Grand Rapids, MI: William B. Eerdmans Publishing Co.
- Brown, C. (1978). *Dictionary of New Testament Theology* (3 vols). Grand Rapids, MI: Zondervan.
- Santala, R. (1992). *The Messiah in the Old Testament.* Jerusalem: Keren Ahvah Meshihit.
- Santala, R. (1993). *The Messiah in the New Testament in the Light of Rabbinical Writings.* Jerusalem: Keren Ahvah Meshihit.
- *Encyclopedia Judaica*. Jerusalem: Keter Publishing House.

- Rambsel, Y. (1996). *Yeshua.* Toronto: Frontier Research Publications.
- Stern, D. H. (1989). *Jewish New Testament.* Jerusalem: Jewish New Testament Publications.

Other Resources

- Bullinger, E.W. (1964). *The Companion Bible.* Grand Rapids, MI: Zondervan.
- Larkin, C. (1918). *Dispensational Truth.* Glendale, PA: Larkin Estate.
- Lindsey, H. (1989). *Road to Holocaust.* New York: Bantam Books, NY.
- Edersheim, A. (1958). *The Temple, Its Ministry and Services.* Grand Rapids, MI: William B. Eerdmans Publishing Co.
- Riplinger, G.A. (1993). *New Age Bible Versions.* Munroe Falls, OH: A.V. Publications.
- Geisler, N. L. (1980). *Inerrancy.* Grand Rapids, MI: Zondervan.

How We Got Our Bible

- Where did our Bible come from? How good are the texts?
- Why do we believe its origin is supernatural?
- How do we know that it really is the Word of God?
- How accurate are our translations?
- Which version is the best?

Chuck Missler, an internationally recognized Biblical authority, reviews the origin of both the Old and New Testaments in light of recent discoveries and controversies.

How We Got Our Bible

DR. CHUCK MISSLER

 Available from https://Resources.khouse.org

Hidden Treasures

For the novice as well as the sophisticate, this book is full of surprises. It includes subtle discoveries lying just "beneath" the text – hidden messages, encryptions, deliberate misspellings and other amendments to the text – that present implications beyond the immediate context, demonstrating a skillful design that has its origin from outside our space and time. Drawing upon over forty years of collecting, Chuck highlights in this book many of the precious nuggets that have become characteristic of his popular Bible studies around the world.

It is guaranteed to stimulate, provoke, and, hopefully, to disturb. It will confound the skeptic and encourage the believer. It is a "must read" for every thinking seeker of truth and serious inquirer of reality.

Endnotes

1 2 Timothy 3:16

2 Ephesians 6:17

3 Villa, P., Roebroeks,W. (2014) Neandertal Demise: An Archaeological Analysis of the Modern Human Superiority Complex. *PLOS ONE* 9(4): e96424

4 James 1:17

5 Hebrews 13:8

6 Scholars offer many drawn-out dating schemes for the Old Testament. To find the date of Isaac's near-sacrifice, we can do simple Bible math. Adding king reigns from the destruction of the Temple in 586 B.C. to Solomon's reign puts Solomon's 4th year in 1015 B.C. Solomon's 4th year was 480 years after the Exodus (1 Kings 6:1). The Exodus took place 430 years after Jacob's family went down into Egypt (Exodus 12:40, 41). Jacob moved to Egypt at age 130, living there 17 years until he died at 147 (Genesis 47:28). Isaac was sixty when Jacob and Esau were born (Genesis 25:26). According to Josephus in The Antiquities of the Jews (1.13.2), Isaac was almost-sacrificed by Abraham when he was 25 (35 years before the twins were born). This basic math places the Akedah, the near-sacrifice of Isaac, in 2090 B.C.

7 Psalm 90:4; 2 Peter 3:8

8 Fulfilling a wide variety of prophesies, notably: 2 Thessalonians 2:3-4; Daniel 7:24-25; 9:27; Revelation 13:5-8

9 Job 26:8; 36:27-28; 38:33-34

10 Leviticus 25:2-5

11 Leviticus 18:6-13

12 Leviticus 11, 13, 15; Numbers 19, Deuteronomy 23:12-13

13 Physicists currently believe there are 11 dimensions in the universe. For more information, see chapter 3 of our book *Beyond Time and Space* (2016).

14 Revelation 21:6; 22:13

15 Please see our study, *Daniel's 70 Weeks.*

16 2 Corinthians 5:21

17 Genesis 22:14

18 2 Peter 3:9

19 2 Timothy 3:16

20 Krucoff, C. (January 29, 1984). The 6 O'Clock Scholar: Librarian of Congress Daniel Boorstin And His Love Affair With Books. *The Washington Post,* page K8, column 2.

21 Deuteronomy 11:16; Job 15:31; Luke 21:8; 1 Corinthians 6:9; 15:33; Galatians 6:7

22 John 6:32-35

23 1 Corinthians 10:4

24 John 4:13-14

25 John 1:29

26 Isaiah 11:1; Jeremiah 23:5; 33:15; John 15:4

27 Psalm 118:22-23; Matthew 21:42; Ephesians 2:20

28 Isaiah 53:2

29 Songs 5:16

30 Josephus, F. (A.D. 94) *Antiquities of the Jews*, 18.3.3.

31 Eusebius (340). *Ecclesiastical History.* 2.25.5-8.

32 Acts 12:2

33 Foxe, J. (1563). *Foxe's Book of Martyrs.* 1.13.

34 Matthew 26:39b

35 Luke 22:44

36 Burgon, J. (1990). *Unholy hands on the Bible* (pp. C41-42) (J. Green, Ed.). Lafayette, Ind.: Sovereign Grace Trust Fund.

37 *Ibid*, p. C-42.

38 Kitchen, K. (1965). The Aramaic of Daniel. In D. J. Wiseman (Ed.), *Notes on Some Problems in the Book of Daniel* (p. 79). London: The Tyndale Press.

39 Kitchen, K. (1965). The Aramaic of Daniel. In D. J. Wiseman (Ed.), *Notes on Some Problems in the Book of Daniel* (p. 77). London: The Tyndale Press.

40 Matthew 24:15; 26:64; Mark 13:14, 26; Daniel 7:13-14; 9:27; 11:31; 12:11

41 1 Peter 1:20; Revelation 13:8

42 I was not a young student of the Bible in the 19th century, just in case you wanted to ask. I had to wait until the late 1940s for that honor.

43 Isaiah 2:8, 18, 20; 10:10-11; 30:22; 31:7; 40:19-20; 44:9-19; 45:16; 57:5

44 Isaiah 1:9-15; 5:7-11; 32:5-7; 33:14-16; 56:10-12; 59:1-4, 7-8, 13

45 Isaiah 13; 14; 21:1-9; 47

46 Isaiah 7:14; 9:1-7; 11:1-10; 42:1-7; 49:6; 52:13; 53-12; 61:1-3

47 Isaiah 1:26-27; 10:21-22; 12:1-6; 14:1-3; 25:1-9; 27:6, 12-13; 35:1-10; 44:28; 45:17, 25; 49:6, 13-23; 51:3; 66:13

48 Allis, O. (1951). *The Unity of Isaiah* (p. 40). Eugene, OR: Wipf and Stock.

49 Isaiah 44:26

50 Matthew 23:23

51 Rauhala, E. (2014, October 21). Risen Again: China's Underground Churches. *Time*.

About the Author

Chuck Missler
President/Founder,
Koinonia House

Chuck Missler was raised in Southern California.

Chuck demonstrated an aptitude for technical interests as a youth. He became a ham radio operator at age nine and started piloting airplanes as a teenager. While still in high school, Chuck built a digital computer in the family garage.

His plans to pursue a doctorate in electrical engineering at Stanford University were interrupted when he received a Congressional appointment to the United States Naval Academy at Annapolis. Graduating with honors, Chuck took his commission in the Air Force. After completing flight training, he met and married Nancy (who later founded The King's High Way ministry). Chuck joined the Missile Program and eventually became Branch Chief of the Department of Guided Missiles.

Chuck made the transition from the military to the private sector when he became a systems engineer with TRW, a large aerospace firm. He then went on to serve as a senior analyst with a non-profit think tank where he conducted projects for the intelligence community and the Department of Defense. During that time, Chuck earned a master's degree in engineering at UCLA, supplementing previous graduate work in applied mathematics, advanced statistics and information sciences.

Recruited into senior management at the Ford Motor Company in Dearborn, Michigan, Chuck established the first international computer network in 1966. He left Ford to start his own company, a computer network firm that was subsequently acquired by Automatic Data Processing (listed on the New York Stock Exchange) to become its Network Services Division.

As Chuck notes, his day of reckoning came in the early '90s when — as the result of a merger — he found himself the chairman and a major shareholder of a small, publicly owned development company known as Phoenix Group International. The firm established an $8 billion joint venture with the Soviet Union to supply personal computers to their 143,000 schools. Due to several unforeseen circumstances, the venture failed. The Misslers lost everything, including their home, automobiles and insurance.

It was during this difficult time that Chuck turned to God and the Bible. As a child he had developed an intense interest in the Bible; studying it became a favorite pastime. In the 1970s, while still in the corporate world, Chuck began leading weekly Bible studies at the 30,000 member Calvary Chapel Costa Mesa, in California. He and Nancy established Koinonia House in 1973, an organization devoted to encouraging people to study the Bible.

Chuck had enjoyed a longtime, personal relationship with Hal Lindsey, who upon hearing of Chuck's professional misfortune, convinced him that he could easily succeed as an independent author and speaker. Over the years, Chuck had developed a loyal following. (Through Doug Wetmore, head of the tape ministry of Firefighters for Christ, Chuck learned that over 7 million copies of his taped Bible studies were scattered throughout the world.) Koinonia House then became Chuck's full-time profession.

Include a Psalm in the front end or the back end of your study time

Also besides serious study time just bath in the words reading right on through God speaks to you through his word ex: 3 chapters a day

Chuck
book mark in the Torah - uses Joshua as a
book mark in the Historical Books
book mark in the poetical Books
book mark in the Prophits
book mark in the Gospils
using Acts as a Gospile
tries to move each bookmark 1 chapt a day

The movie Encounter - Jesus says if you want to love you have to abandon hate Don't let anger steal your joy.

If you don't let go of anger and resentment it will poison every relationship you have even the one with Him